I'M SAVED! NOW WHERE DO I GO FROM HERE?

SANDRA (LOTT) SMITH

I'M SAVED! NOW WHERE DO I GO FROM HERE?

Fourth Edition

Note: Pictures are strictly models and names and places in this book in no way represent in real person or place. The places, events, and people are strictly fictitious.

 www.yournewlifeministries.org

Published in the United States of America by
Your New Life Ministries LLC

CONTENTS

Introduction

Congratulations! You have either just received Jesus as your personal Lord and Savior or you are strongly contemplating doing so. It is the single most important decision you will ever make. Our life here on earth is but a breath and then it is over. "Man's days are determined; you have decreed the number of his months and have set limits he cannot exceed," (Job 14:5).

Where you will spend eternity is entirely up to you. God is gentle and humble in heart. "Come to me, all you who are weary and burdened, and I will give you rest. Take my yoke upon you and learn from me, for I am gentle and humble in heart, and you will find rest for your souls. For My yoke is easy and my burden is light," (Matt. 11:28-30). He will lead and guide you, convict you, but will not force Himself on you. He is not a dictator, but a loving God who died for your sins! "Dear friends, let us love one another, for love comes from God. This is how God showed His love among us: He sent His One and Only Son into the world so that we might live through Him. This is love: not that we loved God, but that He loved us and sent His Son as an atoning sacrifice for our sins," (John 4:7 and 9-10). Salvation is a free gift; He already paid the price, and all you have to do is receive it by faith.

In the pages of this book, you will find Bible studies to help you understand what it means to be saved and to help you begin your Christian walk. You will find studies to help you in your spiritual growth and learn about spiritual warfare and how to be blessed by God. Unfortunately, God does not promise us a *walk-in-the-park* life after we are born again. Satan still very much exists, and he roams the earth doing what he can to deter people from receiving Christ and destroy their walk with Him once they do. "Humble yourselves, therefore, under God's mighty hand, that He may lift you up in due time. Cast all your anxiety on Him because He cares for you. Be self-controlled and alert. Your enemy the devil prowls around like a roaring lion looking for someone to devour. Resist him, standing firm in the faith, because you know that your brothers throughout the world are undergoing the same kind of suffering. And the God of all grace, who called you to His eternal glory in Christ, after you have suffered a little while, will Himself restore you and make you strong, firm, and steadfast. To Him be the power forever and ever. Amen," (1 Peter 5:6-11)

It may not be easy but remember why you received Jesus in the first place: to save your soul. Eternity is forever and where you spend it is entirely up to you; life on earth is just preparation for where we will spend it. Take heart, dear child of God, he has you covered! That is why we have the Bible; it is our spiritual food. The Bible is to our spirit as food is to our body, and without either one we will be weak. "I am the bread of life. He who comes to me will never go hungry, and he who believes in me will never be thirsty," (John 6:35). Stay in the Word, and God, through the Holy Spirit, will lead you, guide you, and teach you.

As you read, scriptures will jump off the page and catch your attention if God is trying to tell you something through it. You will learn how to live a godly life and grow closer to God. The whole Bible fits together for our good and our protection, to help us through life, and we are to follow all His commands. "See that you do all I command you; do not add to it or take away from it," (Deuteronomy 12:32). All of it is true. "Sanctify them by the truth; your word is truth," (John 17:17). It is all from God to bless us. "All Scripture is God-breathed and is useful for teaching, rebuking, correcting and training in righteousness, so that the man of God may be thoroughly equipped for every good work," (2 Tim. 3:16-17). The Word of God was given to us to bless us and to help us go through life with all the love and encouragement that God can give us.

"Praise the Lord. Blessed is the man who fears the Lord, who finds great delight in His commands," (Psalm 112:1)

CHAPTER 1

Salvation: The First Step

You have received Jesus as your personal Lord and Savior! Rejoice! That is the single most important decision you will ever make. But in case you still have some questions, below are a few verses to read and dwell on in your heart. Let the Holy Spirit of God bring you clarity to whatever doubts you may have. I am sure you will want to pray the Invitation Prayer following. Take a few moments and read through these Scriptures and let God talk to your heart, then we will get back to the process of beginning your journey with Christ.

GOD LOVES YOU!

Jeremiah 31:3 "I have loved you with an everlasting love; I have drawn you with loving-kindness"

1 Timothy 2:3-4 "God our Savior, who wants all men to be saved and to come to the knowledge of the truth."

He will not knock on the door of your heart forever. Will you let him in?

Revelation 3:20 "Here I am! I stand at the door and knock. If anyone hears my voice and opens the door, I will come in and eat with him, and he with me."

Jesus is the *only* way to God.

John 14:6 "I am the way, the truth, and the life. No one comes to the Father except through me."

John 3:3 "I tell you the truth, no one can see the kingdom of God unless he is born again."

And you must make Him Lord of your life.

Matthew 6:24 "No one can serve two masters."

Matthew 7:21 "Not everyone who says to me, 'Lord,' will enter the kingdom of heaven, but only he who does the will of My Father who is in heaven."

We must leave our old ways behind.

Mark 3:25 "If a house is divided against itself, that house cannot stand."

You can't live according to the flesh and desires of the sinful nature and expect to have Jesus in your heart. He is holy. He is love. Love and hate cannot exist together.

Ephesians 4:22-24 "You were taught, with regard to your former way of life, to put off your old self, which is being corrupted by its deceitful desires; to be made new in the attitude of your minds; and to put on the new self, created to be like God in true righteousness and holiness."

God gives you the ability to do his will. He knows it is hard.

Philippians 4:13 "I can do everything through Him who gives me strength."

Romans 3:23 "For all have sinned and fall short of the glory of God."

John 1:9 "If we confess our sins, He is faithful and just and will forgive us our sins and purify us from all unrighteousness."

John 1:12 "Yet to all who received Him, to those who believed in His name, He gave the right to become children of God."

Romans 10:10 "For it is with your heart that you believe and are justified, and it is with your mouth that you confess and are saved."

After you confess and ask forgiveness and receive Jesus into your heart, you must *testify* (tell someone) and be baptized. In this, God is glorified, and others might be saved by your example.

2 Tim. 1:8 "So do not be ashamed to testify about our Lord."

1 Peter 3:21 "And this water symbolizes baptism that now saves you also not the removal of dirt from the body but the pledge of a good conscience toward God. It saves you by the resurrection of Jesus Christ."

Invitation to Salvation Prayer

Dear Almighty Father in heaven, I know that I am a sinner, and I ask your forgiveness of all my sins. I want to make you the Lord of my life and I want to serve you all the days of my life. I believe that Jesus Christ died on the cross for my sins. Thank you so much for loving me and waiting for me to come to the knowledge of the truth! Thank you for my salvation. Please help me and guide me in learning your word so I can be a light to the world. Please, Jesus, come into my heart and baptize me with your Holy Spirit. I thank you and praise your Holy Name and ask all this in the name of Jesus Christ our Lord. Amen.

I am sure you have been convinced; for in reaching for this book, the Holy Spirit has already been dealing with your heart. So, now I can say it again: congratulations and welcome to the family of God! The rest of this book consists of different Bible studies the Lord has given me to help me begin my spiritual walk; they helped me, and I know they will help you as well. To put it very simply, you need to stay in the Word. Jesus is the word and all of who he is—is written in the Bible. "In the beginning was the Word, and the Word was with God, and the Word was God. He was with God in the beginning," (John 1:1-2). The Word of God is Jesus Christ. "The Word became flesh and made His dwelling among us. We have seen His glory, the glory of the One and only, who came from the Father, full of grace and truth," (John 1:14). God's word, the Bible, and Jesus Christ will sustain us through life if we trust in him. "The Son is the radiance of God's glory and the exact representation of His being, sustaining all things by His powerful Word," (Hebrews 1:3). The world was dark before God gave it light. That is how we all live before we accept Jesus Christ - we live in darkness. The darkness of our heart fills our spirits.

Accepting Jesus as your personal Lord and Savior will bring light to your heart and spirit. "I am the light of the world. Whoever follows me will never walk in darkness but will have the light of life," (John 8:12). Since the Word was first and Jesus was the Word, accepting him will bring to life everything in the Bible that you read. What you once read before and did not understand, Jesus will bring to life in your heart. You will not only understand it, but it will have great meaning to you. Before coming to Jesus, understanding the Bible is difficult to do for *unbelievers* because of Satan. He does not want you to understand it so that he can keep you from getting closer to God. Only God can take the blinders off; this only happens upon repentance. "The god of this age has blinded the minds of unbelievers, so they cannot see the light of the gospel, of the glory of Christ, who is the image of God," (2 Corinthians 4:4). Upon repentance, God takes the blinders off and enlightens your heart with the Spirit of Christ, which brings peace and understanding to your soul. "Be ever hearing, but never understanding; be ever seeing, but never perceiving. Make the heart of this people calloused; make their ears dull and close their eyes. Otherwise, they might see with their eyes, hear with their ears, understand with their hearts, and turn and be healed," (Isaiah 6:9-10).

Here are a few steps to a victorious journey in Christ:

1. Repent of sin
2. Ask Jesus into your heart
3. Find a good Church

Ask the Lord to lead you to the right one. Going to church will not save you in any way, but fellowshipping with other believers is something we are called to do. "Let us not give up meeting together, as some are in the habit of doing, but let us encourage one another all the more as you see the day approaching," (Hebrews 10:25). We meet others who can also help us and be a comfort to us when we need to talk to someone. Godly counsel from a fellow believer, one who may have been through some of the same things, will help you along the way. "Praise be to the God and Father of our Lord Jesus Christ, the Father of compassion and the God of all comfort, who comforts us in all our troubles so that we can comfort those in any trouble with the comfort we ourselves have received from God," (2 Corinthians 1:3-4).

4. Get baptized

"And this water symbolizes baptism that now saves you also not the removal of dirt from the body but the pledge of a good conscience toward God. It saves you by the resurrection of Jesus Christ," (1 Peter 3:21).

5. Stay, stay, stay in the Word!

It is your strength to walk through victoriously! "I am the vine; you are the branches. If a man remains in me, and I in him, he will bear much fruit; apart from me you can do nothing," (John 15:5).

6. Communicate with God daily

Any relationship that grows and flourishes takes effort; it takes spending time with the other person. If you never talk to your spouse or friends, if you never do anything with them, those relationships will not last very long. To grow closer to God you need to spend time with him not only in prayer asking for what is on your heart but talking to him. The more time you spend with God (talking to him, reading the Word, and studying the Bible) the closer you will become; you will feel his presence more and more. If you want a deeper relationship with God, you cannot expect him to carry all responsibility.

"Submit yourselves, then, to God. Resist the devil, and he will flee from you. Come near to God and He will come near to you," (James 4:7-8).

Am I Saved? And What Does That Mean?

Have you already prayed to Lord Jesus to be saved, but do not know if you are? First, if you spend all your time fearing that you aren't saved, tell God about it. He wants you to tell him everything - the smaller the better because you already know your Father wants you to tell him the big stuff. He likes you to tell him the small thoughts (bad or good) as well. Don't you want to know everything that goes on in your children's lives?

Second, that fear of not being saved can be used for good. Did you ever think about that? Fear is a powerful emotion; why else would you be in so much pain and confusion? Use that fear not to worry about salvation, but to seek God's love and peace. Just assume that you are saved if you have already asked him. Ask God to open your eyes to see the ways that he is showing his love for you in your life; that assumption is a powerful force. When you take the next step and act on your assumption, it is called faith, and God your Father ALWAYS honors the faith of his children. Although, (to ease your concerns) if you asked Jesus into your heart, then yes. "To those who received Him, to those who believed in His name, He gave the right to become children of God." (John 1:12) You are saved!

Still wondering what 'being saved' means?

To be saved means to know without a doubt that your eternal home will be in heaven. The only way is through Jesus Christ.

John 10:9 "I am the gate; whoever enters through me will be saved."

John 14:6 "I am the way and the truth and the life. No one comes to the Father except through me."

Psalm 68:20 "Our God is a God who saves; from the Sovereign Lord comes escape from death."

Acts 4:12 "Salvation is found in no one else, for there is no other name under heaven given to men by which we must be saved."

In reading this information about what it means to be saved, ask yourself what the most important thing in your life is. What do you put first in your life, and what do you do that you just cannot live without? If it is not God, then it is your *idol*. An idol, according to Webster's New American Dictionary, is anything that you give excessive love or devotion to. Where does your devotion lie? Are you still wondering if you are saved? Have you asked Jesus into your heart, but have not experienced any change of heart? Do you still get drunk and do drugs? Do you still have a problem with cigarettes, or overeating? Are you a shopaholic or a workaholic? Do you have a problem with lust and pornography or a mouth that can't keep itself out of other people's affairs or from spreading news about them? Do you have emotional problems such as anger, impatience, rebellion, or forgiveness that seem to control you? An idol is anything that has control over you or has mastered you. That should only be God.

Here is an activity to help you understand your heart and be filled with the Holy Spirit:

Get a cup and picture your heart as a cup. Now, get some seeds (or something you can use as seeds) and paper and write on it the different emotions or addictions that have consumed you (e.g. alcohol, drug addiction, nicotine addiction, anger, rage, bitterness, selfishness, pride, lack of forgiveness, etc.). Put the seeds in the bottom of the cup. The seeds represent the fruit of the Spirit. Ball the paper up and put it in the cup. Now, ask yourself where is there room for the fruit of the Spirit to grow.

As you can see, there isn't room - that is where trials come in. You can say, "I am not going to get angry or go to bars." It may work for a while, but it is an issue that may have been caused by something else; you have to get to the root of the issue, or you will continue to have the same problem. God knows your heart better than you do. He created it. He will change you from the inside out, little by little. You love, believe in him, trust him, and obey him and he will change you. That is what his grace and love is all about.

James 1:2-5 "Consider it pure joy, my brothers, whenever you face trials of many kinds because you know that the testing of your faith develops perseverance. Perseverance must finish its work so that you may be mature and complete, not lacking anything. If any of you lacks wisdom, he should ask God, who gives generously to all without finding fault, and it will be given to him."

2 Corinthians 5:17 "Therefore, if anyone is in Christ, he is a new creation; the old has gone, the new has come!"

Deuteronomy 7:22 "The Lord your God will drive out those nations before you, little by little. You will not be allowed to eliminate them all at once, or the wild animals will multiply around you."

1 Peter 2:19 "For a man is a slave to whatever has mastered him."

Exodus 20:3-4 "You shall have no other gods before me. You shall not make for yourself an idol in the form of anything in heaven above or on the earth beneath or in the waters below."

Proverbs 23:19-21 "Listen, my son, and be wise, and keep your heart on the right path. Do not join those who drink too much wine or gorge themselves on meat, for drunkards and gluttons become poor, and drowsiness clothes them in rags."

Proverbs 23:29-35 "Who has woe? Who has sorrow? Who has strife? Who has complaints? Who has bloodshot eyes? Those who linger over wine, who go to sample bowls of mixed wine. Do not gaze at wine when it is red, when it sparkles in the cup when it goes down smoothly! In the end, it bites like a snake and poisons like a viper. Your eyes will see strange sights and your mind imagines confusing things. You will be like one sleeping on the high seas, lying on top of the rigging. 'They hit me,' you will say, 'but I'm not hurt! They beat me, but I don't feel it! When will I wake up so I can find another drink?"

What if I worship idols? What if I don't want to quit smoking cigarettes, doing drugs, or drinking alcohol, but I still want to be saved and be right with God? What do I do? Pray to Jesus acknowledging that he alone has the power to get you right with God. If you could do it alone, you wouldn't need God, would you? Tell Jesus that you believe in him and that he is your risen Lord. Tell him that you want to walk in the Spirit but cannot or do not want to quit your addictions. The Apostle Paul admits his struggles in the book of Romans. Be straight with God. He does not want you to sugarcoat the truth. He is truth, and he detests lying whether it is to someone else or yourself - lying is still lying. He already knows your heart. He just wants you to ask. If you have sinned, tell God about it. Tell him how your desire to sin is greater than your desire to quit (this is true or you would have already quit), but you still want him to give you salvation. God will honor your honesty by listening and answering your prayers. The first step to receiving the salvation God so badly desires to give you is admitting what you are doing or desiring is a sin. By simply admitting that to yourself, you have taken the biggest step!!!

Now comes the easy part. Admit it to the Lord. I say this is easy because he already knows; all he wants, and needs is for you to tell him. As I said before, God will change you. You must stop going to the bars, buying cigarettes, etc. as an act of faith that God will do the rest. Trust him as you obey his word. He will change your heart and take those desires away, healing you in the process.

Romans 7:18-20 "I know that nothing good lives in me, that is, in my sinful nature. For I have the desire to do what is good, but I cannot carry it out. For what I do is not the good I want to do; no, the evil I do not want to do—this I keep on doing. Now if I do what I do not want to do, it is no longer I who do it, but it is sin living in me that does it."

Romans 7:24-25 "What a wretched man I am! Who will rescue me from this body of death? Thanks be to God—through Jesus Christ our Lord!"

James 4:2 "You do not have, because you do not ask God."

John 4:24 "God is spirit, and His worshipers must worship I spirit and in truth."

Proverbs 12:22 "The Lord detests lying lips, but He delights in men who are truthful."

John 3:20 "For God is greater than our hearts, and He knows everything."

Psalm 139:4 "Before a word is on my tongue you know it completely, O Lord."

"God, I know that doing *this* (or desiring *this*) is a sin against you, but I do not have the power to quit or stop wanting it. I know that you can take care of those sins and give me the desires that are okay. I did my part by telling you about it now, do your thing and help me and save me. I am willing to obey you so give me the power to do so. Give me Your Holy Spirit Lord Jesus. Without it living and acting inside of me, I realize that I cannot obey God like I need to, like I want to. Please help me, save me, fill me, and baptize me with Your Holy Spirit!"

After you pray that to God and actually mean it, you can rest assured that you are saved. How will you know that you are saved? You will know by the Holy Spirit who will confirm it to you in your heart. If you haven't received the baptism yet - relax. It may take time but keep seeking Him. "Do not leave Jerusalem, but wait for the gift My Father promised, which you have heard me speak about. For John baptized with water, but in a few days, you will be baptized with the Holy Spirit" **(Acts 1:4-5).** That keeps God on your mind and lets Him know that you really want it. Keep seeking Him and you WILL find Him when you seek Him with ALL YOUR HEART.

How important is God to you?

Another thing to ponder as you think about these things is how important is God to you. How important is obeying Him and doing His will to you? How important is reading His Word to you? Jesus is the Word and reading it is like putting more and more of Him into you. He is the one who gives you strength and peace. He is the One who overcame and it is only through Him that we can overcome every trial as well. Are you truly sorry for the sins you have committed? Be honest because God knows the secrets of the heart. You cannot hide the truth from God; He already knows it no matter how much you may try to convince yourself otherwise. God already knows.

Psalm 44:20-21 "If we had forgotten the name of our God or spread out our hands to a foreign god, would not God have discovered it since He knows the secrets of the heart?"

If you have not truly turned from your old life of sin when you asked Jesus into your heart, then it is not true repentance. It is just lip service.

Isaiah 29:13 "These people come near to me with their mouth and honor me with their lips, but their hearts are far from me."

John 3:6 "No one who continues to sin has either seen Him or knows Him."

John 3:9 "No one who is born of God will continue to sin, because God's seed remains in him; he cannot go on sinning, because he has been born of God."

Ephesians 4:22-24 "You were taught, with regard to your former way of life, to put off your old self, which is being corrupted by its deceitful desires; to be made new in the attitude of your minds; and to put on the new self, created to be like God in true righteousness and holiness."

Is your life one of habitual sin and consistent turmoil?

Is your life consistently in turmoil and full of continued habitual sin? Do you keep running after habits or emotions (idols) that you just cannot break? Where do you run to for your peace and joy? Do you run to God or your neighborhood bar or drug dealer? Do you run back to work or to the mall to buy something that you really do not have the money for or do you run to the refrigerator to eat when you really aren't hungry? Who do you seek rest, love, and comfort for your soul from? Is it God or your habits? Loving people is not wrong; we are called to "Love your neighbor as yourself." That is why God made Adam and Eve. So we would have someone to share our life with, but when you leave God out, the One who created you and keeps you breathing and can give you either an eternal life in heaven or hell is when it is wrong.

Psalm 29:11 "The Lord gives strength to His people; the Lord blesses His people with peace."

God's peace is eternal. The world's peace is temporary.
God is Spirit; He is eternal. He is love and His love and peace will last forever.

2 Corinthians 4:18 "For what is seen is temporary, but what is unseen is eternal."

John 4:7-8 "Dear friends, let us love one another, for love comes from God. Everyone who loves has been born of God and knows God. Whoever does not love does not know God, because God is love."

Psalm 21:6 "Surely you have granted him eternal blessings and made him glad with the joy of your presence."

Habakkuk 3:6 "His ways are eternal."

Proverbs 16:7 "When a man's ways are pleasing to the Lord, He makes even his enemies live at peace with him."

God is supernatural. God is eternal and so is His peace and joy!

So, now you know that God's peace and joy are eternal. The things of this earth which are natural things that you can see and touch, only give you temporary peace.

John 2:17 "The world and its desires pass away, but the man who does the will of God lives forever."

The things of this earth do not heal the problems that are in our lives and hearts. They only give temporary relief. The problem is still there. Antidepressants give you masked joy. They don't get to the root issue and heal it. God does. God heals and He heals it completely. I don't know about you but when I have a problem, I want it gone for good, not temporarily until the "high" from whatever earthly thing that I have taken or done wears off!

Matthew 15:13 "Every plant that my heavenly Father has not planted will be pulled up by the roots."

Jeremiah 30:17 "But I will restore you to health and heal your wounds, declares the Lord."

Jeremiah 2:28 "Where then are the gods you made for yourselves? Let them come if they can save you when you are in trouble! For you have as many gods as you have towns, O Judah."

What is your idol? What are you giving excessive devotion to? The idols that you have in your life will not save you nor will they heal and deliver you from the troubles that you have. Only God does that.

Psalm 146:4 "The sorrows of those will increase who run after other gods."

Jonah 2:8 "Those who cling to worthless idols forfeit the grace that could be theirs."

Examine your ways. It is better for you to examine yourself and confess to God than for God to change you through trials!

2 Corinthians 13:5 "Examine yourselves to see whether you are in the faith; test yourselves."

John 1:9 "If we confess our sins, He is faithful and just and will forgive us our sins and purify us from all unrighteousness."

What idols do you have? Are you overwhelmed with a gossiping mouth, filthy language, sexual immorality, lying, hatred (racism is a form of hatred), jealousy, envy, greed selfish ambition, etc.? Emotions and things that you do, if you become obsessed with them and will not repent, can be an idol as well.

Galatians 5:19-21 "The acts of the sinful nature are obvious: sexual immorality, impurity, and debauchery; idolatry and witchcraft; hatred, discord, jealousy, fits of rage, selfish ambition, dissensions, factions, and envy; drunkenness, orgies, and the like. I warn you, as I did before, that those who live like this will not inherit the kingdom of God."

Ephesians 5:3-7 "But among you there must not be even a hint of sexual immorality, or of any kind of impurity, or of greed, because these are improper for God's holy people. Nor should there be obscenity, foolish talk, or coarse joking, which are out of place, but rather thanksgiving. For of this, you can be sure: No immoral, impure, or greedy person—such a man is an idolater—has any inheritance in the kingdom of Christ and of God. Let no one deceive you with empty words, for because of such things God's wrath comes on those who are disobedient. Therefore, do not partner with them."

Colossians 3:5-11 Put to death, therefore, whatever belongs to your earthly nature: sexual immorality, impurity, lust, evil desires, and greed, which is idolatry. Because of these, the wrath of God is coming. You used to walk in these ways, in the life you once lived. But now you must rid yourselves of all such things as these: anger, rage, malice, slander, and filthy language from your lips. Do not lie to each other, since you have taken off your old self with its practices and have put on the new self, which is being renewed in knowledge in the image of its Creator. Here there is no Greek or Jew, circumcised or uncircumcised, barbarian, Scythian, slave or free, but Christ is all, and is in all."

John 3:15 "Anyone who hates his brother is a murderer, and you know that no murderer has eternal life in Him."

To murder someone can be physical in taking someone's life or it can be emotionally or spiritually. Words and actions can destroy a person emotionally and spiritually; they do hurt. They can either tear down or build up.

Proverbs 12:18 "Reckless words pierce like a sword, but the tongue of the wise brings healing."

Proverbs 16:24 "Pleasant words are a honeycomb, sweet to the soul and healing to the bones."

James 3:8-10 "With the tongue we praise our Lord and Father, and with it, we curse men, who have made in God's likeness. Out of the same mouth come praise and cursing."

God shows no favoritism. All who disobey and reject Jesus will reap what they sow. If you sow into the sinful desires and to the world, destruction is what you will reap, eternally and physically to your heart and soul and eventually your life on earth. If you sow spiritually to

God, you will reap eternal life in your heart and soul while on earth and in the life to come.

Acts 10:34-35 "I now realize how true it is that God does not show favoritism but accepts men from every nation who fear Him and do what is right."

Galatians 6:7-8 "Do not be deceived: God cannot be mocked. A man reaps what he sows. The one who sows to please his sinful nature, from that nature will reap destruction; the one who sows to please the Spirit, from the Spirit will reap eternal life."

Truthfully examine yourself and then ask yourself again, "Am I saved?" God truly knows. He knows your heart. If you are not sure then, as I have said earlier, pray and take it to God. Tell Him the addictions, habits, or other problems that have a hold on you. Tell Him why you do them and ask Him to show you what to do to be saved. All sins are forgiven. All you have to do is ask. Many people think that they have to be perfect to come to God. Not so! People who are well do not seek out a doctor; only those who are sick. So, it is with God. Seek Him and He will do the cleaning up. You just need to sincerely come to Him and ask!!

Matthew 9:12-13 "It is not the healthy who need a doctor, but the sick. But go and learn what this means: 'I desire mercy, not sacrifice.' For I have not come to call the righteous, but sinners."

John 17:17 "Sanctify them by the truth, your word is truth."

Psalm 51:10 "Create in me a pure heart, O God, and renew a steadfast spirit within me."

1 Timothy 2:3-4 "God our Savior, who wants all men to be saved and to come to a knowledge of the truth."

Psalm 103:2-3 "Praise the Lord, O my soul, and forget not all His benefits—who forgives all your sins and heals all your diseases."

God knows lip service. He knows if you are sincere. Your actions will find you out. If you have truly made Jesus the Lord of your life you will love and obey Him.

Matthew 7:13 "By their fruit you will recognize them."

Matthew 7:21 "Not everyone who says to me, 'Lord, Lord,' will enter into the kingdom of heaven, but only he who does the will of My Father who is in heaven."

Proverbs 21:2 "All a man's ways seem right to him, but the Lord weighs the heart."

Sin alienates you from God

Sin will alienate you from God. He is holy and cannot look on sin. You can only have one master, the things of this world or God. You cannot serve two masters.

Matthew 6:24 "No one can serve two masters. Either he will hate the one and love the other, or he will be devoted to the one and despise the other."

Matthew 12:25 "Every kingdom divided against itself will be ruined, and every city or household divided against itself will not stand."

Habakkuk 1:13 "Your eyes are too pure to look on evil; you cannot tolerate wrong."

Colossians 1:21-23 "Once you were alienated from God and were enemies in your minds because of your evil behavior. But now He has reconciled you by Christ's physical body through death to present you holy in His sight, without blemish and free from accusation—if you continue in your faith, established and firm, not moved from the hope held out in the gospel."

1 Corinthians 10:21-22 "You cannot drink the cup of the Lord and the cup of demons too; you cannot have a part in both the Lord's Table and the table of demons. Are we trying to arouse the Lord's jealousy? Are we stronger than He?"

Sin, if not repented, will result in punishment just as you punish your children for acts of disobedience. By your actions here on earth, you will reap what you sow. Your actions show the true confession of whether the Lord is the Lord of your life or not. You choose eternity in heaven or hell by your true confession. Not the confession of your mouth alone, but that from your heart.

Obadiah: 15 "As you have done, it will be done to you; your deeds will return upon your own head."

Philippians 3:18-21 "Many live as enemies of the cross of Christ. Their destiny is destruction, their god is their stomach, and their glory is in their shame. Their mind is on earthly things. But our citizenship is in heaven. And we eagerly await a Savior from there, the Lord Jesus Christ, who, by the power that enables Him to bring everything under His control, will transform our lowly bodies so that they will be like His glorious body."

Deuteronomy 30:19-20 "I have set before you life and death, blessings and curses. Now choose life, so that you and your children may live and that you may love the Lord your God, listen to His voice, and hold fast to Him."

Not submitting to God is rebelling against Him. You cannot rebel against Him and live according to the lustful desires of the world and expect His blessings, either on earth or in the life to come.

1 Samuel 15:22-23 "To obey is better than sacrifice, and to heed is better than the fat of rams. For rebellion is like the sin of divination, and arrogance like the evil of idolatry."

1 Samuel 12:15 "But if you do not obey the Lord, and if you rebel against His commands, His hand will be against you, as it was against your fathers."

If you do not repent it will not only result in punishment here on earth, but eternal punishment as well. That is eternal separation from God; an eternity (that is forever unending) in hell. If you think you have had bad times here, wait until you see hell if you do not repent! Do you really want to take the chance of spending your eternal home in hell?

Psalm 37:37-38 "Consider the blameless, observe the upright; there is a future for the man of peace. But all sinners will be destroyed; the future of the wicked will be cut off."

Isaiah 1:28 "But rebels and sinners will both be broken, and those who forsake the Lord will perish."

Revelation 20:12-15 "And I saw the dead, great and small, standing before the throne, and books were opened. Another book was opened, which is the Book of Life. The dead were judged according to what they had done as recorded in the books. The sea gave up the dead that were in it, and death and Hades gave up the dead that were in them, and each person was judged according to what he had done. Then death and Hades were thrown into the lake of fire. The lake of fire is the second death. If anyone's name was not found written in the Book of Life, he was thrown into the lake of fire."

Revelation 21:6-8 "He said to me: "It is done. I am the Alpha and Omega, the Beginning and the End. To him who is thirsty I will give to drink without cost from the spring of the water of life. He who overcomes will inherit all this, and I will be his God and he will be my son. But the cowardly, the unbelieving, the vile, the murderers, the sexually immoral, those who practice magic arts, the idolaters, and all liars—their place will be in the fiery lake of burning sulfur. This is the second death."

Don't put it off! Only God knows the hour and time of your death! Your time may be short!

Only God knows the hour and time of your death. You may not have until tomorrow. Do you really want to take a chance with the lusts and desires of the world and the way you may think, and put them up against the Word and the will of God? Do you want to take the chance of maybe ending up in hell if your time came tomorrow and you weren't ready?

Job 14:5 "Man's days are determined; you have decreed the number of his months and have set limits he cannot exceed."

Psalm 39:4-5 "Show me, O Lord, my life's end and the number of my days; let me know how fleeting my life is. You have made my days a mere handbreadth; the span of my years is as nothing before you. Each man's life is but a breath."

The second coming of Christ is getting closer and closer and is a day only known to the Father. Shouldn't you be ready?

2 Peter 3:10-13 "But the day of the Lord will come like a thief. The heavens will disappear with a roar; the elements will be destroyed by fire, and the earth and everything in it will be laid bare. Since everything will be destroyed in this way, what kind of people ought you to be? You ought to live holy and godly lives as you look forward to the day of God and speed its coming. That day will bring about the destruction of the heavens by fire, and the elements will melt in the heat. But in keeping with His promise, we are looking forward to a new heaven and a new earth, the home of righteousness."

God will let you go through pure hell on earth, so you won't have to spend eternity in hell. The bad times on earth are nothing compared to the torment of hell. He will let you go down to the pit and come to the end of yourself, so you will look to Him and give your life to Him.

Job 33:29-30 "God does all these things to a man—twice, even three times—to turn back his soul from the pit that the light of life may shine on him."

2 Peter 3:9 "The Lord is not slow in keeping His promise, as some understand slowness. He is patient with you, not wanting anyone to perish, but everyone to come to repentance."

God wants all men to be saved. He does not want anyone to suffer or to perish in hell. That is why He sent Jesus Christ to die for our sins.

Romans 5:8 "But God demonstrates His own love for us in this: While we were still sinners, Christ died for us."

Are you saved? Are you still not sure? Do you want to be sure?

Has this helped you to see yourself more clearly? Are you sure that you are saved? If so, great! If you are still not sure, do you want to be sure now that you know all of this? Do you want to be positive that your eternal home is in heaven? You can be sure. The Holy Spirit within you will testify with your spirit and tell you that you are God's child.

Romans 8:16 "The Spirit Himself testifies with our spirit that we are God's children."

John 3:3 "I tell you the truth, no one can see the kingdom of God unless he is born again."

John 3:5-7 "I tell you the truth, no one can enter the kingdom of God unless he is born of water and the Spirit. Flesh gives birth to flesh, but the Spirit gives birth to spirit. You should not be surprised at my saying, 'You must be born again."

To be born again is to be made new in the attitude of our hearts. When you sincerely receive Jesus as Lord and truly repent of your sins, your heart is made new. You have new desires; desires to read the Bible and to please God. You will have the fruit of the Spirit.

Galatians 5:22-23 "But the fruit of the Spirit is love, joy, peace, patience, kindness, goodness, faithfulness, gentleness and self-control."

Ezekiel 36:26 "I will give you a new heart and put a new spirit in you; I will remove from you your heart of stone and give you a heart of flesh."

How to be saved

1st - You must admit that you are a sinner. Everyone sins. Jesus is the only blameless One. Humble yourself and come to Him.

James 4:6 "God opposes the proud but gives grace to the humble."

Romans 3:23-24 "For all have sinned and fall short of the glory of God and are justified freely by His grace through the redemption that came by Christ Jesus."

Unless it is true, sincere repentance, it is just lip service and is worthless. You must mean it.

Jeremiah 12:2-3 "You are always on their lips but far from their hearts. Yet you know me, O Lord; you see me and test my thoughts about you."

Isaiah 30:15 "In repentance and rest is your salvation; in quietness and trust is your strength."

2 Corinthians 7:10 "Godly sorrow brings repentance that leads to salvation and leaves no regret, but worldly sorrow brings death."

Hebrews 10:22 "Let us draw near to God with a sincere heart in full assurance of faith, having our hearts sprinkled to cleanse us from a guilty conscience and having our bodies washed with pure water."

2nd - You must believe that Jesus died on the cross for your sins and receive (ask) Him into your heart.

Romans 10:10 "For it is with your heart that you believe and are justified, and it is with your mouth that you confess and are saved."

When you admit this and commit your heart to God you then become saved, born again, a child of God!

John 1:12 "Yet to all who received Him, to those who believed in His name, He gave the right to become children of God."

3rd - You must confess. The Word says to confess. So, to show your faith and commitment to God confess your new-found faith to someone and be baptized! He died for you, so be overjoyed and not ashamed to tell someone!

2 Timothy 1:8 "So do not be ashamed to testify about our Lord, or ashamed of me His prisoner."

Mark 8:36-38 "What good is it for a man to gain the whole world, yet forfeit his soul? Or what can a man give in exchange for his soul? If anyone is ashamed of me and My Words in this adulterous and sinful generation, the Son of Man will be ashamed of him when He comes in His Father's glory with the holy angels."

1 Peter 3:21 "And this water symbolizes baptism that now saves you also not the removal of dirt from the body but the pledge of a good conscience toward God. It saves you by the resurrection of Jesus Christ."

Acts 2:38 "Repent and be baptized, every one of you, in the name of Jesus Christ for the forgiveness of your sins. And you will receive the gift of the Holy Spirit."

Romans 3:22 "This righteousness from God comes through faith in Jesus Christ to all who believe."

Ephesians 2:8-9 "For it is by grace you have been saved, through faith - and this not from yourselves, it is a gift of God - not by works so that no one can boast."

What do you do next?

So, you are going to assume you are saved because you asked Him. How do you act on it so you can call it faith? Read about God, read the

Bible, find Christian friends to tell your testimony to, giving your testimony to other believers is not mainly for their benefit but largely for yours. Speaking out to others that God has saved you from yourself and your desire to sin and maybe even the circumstance is not only precious but also powerful. The most important part about being newly saved-newborn- is spending as much time with God as possible. Listen to a Christian radio station while you are at work if possible. Ask the Lord to keep you with Him and to help you spend more time with Him. You are just saved so you can cast every single worry and doubt you have on God. If you doubt not only that you are saved but also if He is even real, *tell him*. In order to help you through your doubts and fears, you *have* to tell him. So, what if He is God and He already knows, you have to tell Him, trusting that He can do something about your doubts and fears. It is so awesome and precious to God when you run to Him with all your doubts and fears, especially if they are about Him. "Dear God, I asked you to save me but I don't feel saved and I don't know if I really even believe in you because I have doubts. Please help me, Jesus."

Think about it. What did you just do by praying to Him? Your action of prayer just told Him that despite your doubts that He even exists, you would still look to Him as your God. Know that God Almighty, Creator of the universe, your Father WILL MOVE HEAVEN to answer a prayer like that. Do you think He wants His baby boy or girl to fall? Do you think He wants His son or daughter to fall to those doubts? He didn't die for you just to lose to a few doubts as soon as you are saved.

1st - You are now called to be holy. You must leave your old lifestyle behind. This does not mean you can keep going to that bar you used to go to or watching those TV programs with a lot of sex and filthy language. After truly being saved, you should not want to anyway.

This is not a "holier than thou" attitude; it simply loves the Lord with all your heart, with all your soul, and with your entire mind. When you do this, you will want to obey His Word and His will. This will keep you from temptation, sinning further, and falling back into the same hell you were delivered out of. As you draw close to God in your daily life of talking to Him and reading His Word, the Holy Spirit in you helps you to be holy.

You must leave your old lifestyle behind. You are a new creation in Christ with a brand-new start and a brand-new heart. If you keep on doing the same things, then the repentance is useless. The sinful nature that is a part of us by nature will creep up but being strong in the Lord and the Word of God, you will have the strength to overcome and not let it rule you.

2 Corinthians 5:17 "Therefore, if anyone is in Christ, He is a new creation."

Galatians 5:16-17 "So I say, live by the Spirit, and you will not gratify the desires of the sinful nature. For the sinful nature desires what is contrary to the Spirit, and the Spirit what is contrary to the sinful nature."

John 14:26 "But the Counselor, the Holy Spirit, whom the Father will send in My name, will teach you all things and will remind you of everything I have said to you."

John 16:13 "But when He, the Spirit of truth comes, He will guide you into all truth. He will not speak on His own; He will speak only what He hears, and He will tell you what is yet to come."

John 14:21 "Whoever has my commands and obeys them, He is the one who loves me. He who loves me will be loved by My Father, and I too will love him and show myself to him."

1 Peter 1:16 "Be holy, because I am holy."

Galatians 5:1 "It is for freedom that Christ has set us free. Stand firm, then, and do not let yourselves be burdened again by a yoke of slavery."

Through Christ, He will keep you firmly rooted and strong; able to resist the devil's attacks. As long as you keep your eyes on Him and not on the things that come your way. You will stay strong. Keep trusting God. He didn't die for you to not let you have victory in every situation. As a child of God, you will be able to say "no" to past addictions and will want to read the Bible and draw closer to God.

Philippians 4:13 "I can do everything through Him who gives me strength."

James 4:7-8 "Submit yourselves, then, to God. Resist the devil, and he will flee from you. Come near to God and He will come near to you."

Proverbs 18:10 "The name of the Lord is a strong tower; the righteous run to it and are safe."

John 15:5 "I am the vine; you are the branches. If a man remains in Me and I in him, he will bear much fruit; apart from Me you can do nothing."

2nd - Get a Bible, read it, and keep reading it.

The Word of God is your strength and weapon against Satan and his attacks. Jesus was the Word who became flesh for us. Jesus when being tempted in the desert by Satan used the Word to fight him off. He stood by the Word that He spoke and defeated Satan. Only through Jesus and His Word can we defeat him as well.

John 1:1-2 "In the beginning was the Word, and the Word was with God, and the Word was God. He was with God in the beginning."

John 1:14 "The Word became flesh and made His dwelling among us. We have seen His glory, the glory of the One and Only who came from the Father, full of grace and truth."

John 6:47-48 "I tell you the truth, he who believes has everlasting life. I am the bread of life."

2 Corinthians 5:21 "God made Him who had no sin to be sin for us, so that in Him we might become the righteousness of God."

John 16:33 "I have told you these things, so that in me you may have peace. In this world, you will have trouble. But take heart! I have overcome the world."

Joshua 1:8 "Do not let the Book of the Law depart from your mouth; meditate on it day and night, so that you may be careful to do everything written in it. Then you will be prosperous and successful."

Psalm 149:6 "May the praise of God be in their mouths and a double-edged sword in their hands."

3rd - Keep your eyes fixed on Jesus. Go to Church, pray, and read the Word.

If you are now looking at Christ and His ways; it cannot be on the world. Keep your eyes fixed on Jesus. Talk to the Lord every day. You should want to. Satan will not sit idly by and let you live a glorious life. He wants to get at God and the only way is through God's children. You had problems before; the only difference now is you are going to heaven for an eternity. Before, you were not. Before you had only yourself to depend on, now you have big brother Jesus and Papa God to come to your rescue!

Psalm 118:6 "The Lord is with me; I will not be afraid. What can man do to me?" Relationships are two ways. He wants to hear from you. If you never talked to your spouse, what kind of relationship do you think you would have?

Hebrews 10:25 "Let us not give up meeting together, as some are in the habit of doing, but let us encourage one another - and all the more as you see the Day approaching."

Hebrews 12:2-3 "Let us fix our eyes on Jesus, the author, and perfecter of our faith, who for the joy set before Him endured the cross, scorning its shame, and sat down at the right hand of the throne of God. Consider Him who endured such opposition from sinful men, so that you will not grow weary and lose heart."

1 Thessalonians 5:16-18 "Be joyful always; pray continually; give thanks in all circumstances, for this is God's will for you in Christ Jesus."

John 2:15-17 "Do not love the world or anything in the world. If anyone loves the world, the love of the Father is not in him. For everything in the world - the cravings of sinful man, the lust of his eyes, and the boasting of what he has and does - comes not from the Father but from the world. The world and its desires pass away, but the man who does the will of God lives forever."

You were considered dead in your sins and now you are alive in Christ! Saved! Born again! Rejoice and praise God!

Colossians 2:13-14 "When you were dead in your sins and in the uncircumcision of your sinful nature, God made you alive with Christ.

He forgave us all our sins, having canceled the written code, with its regulations, that was against us and that stood opposed to us; He took it away, nailing it to the cross."

Jesus Christ is in you now. All things are possible through Him.

Matthew 19:26 "With man this is impossible, but with God all things are possible."

Psalm 60:12 "With God we will gain the victory, and He will trample down our enemies."

Called By God

John 11:43 "Lazarus, come out!" "Take off the grave clothes and let him go."

All who are chosen are predestined by God and called and sealed by the Holy Spirit upon conversion.

Ephesians 1:4-6 "For He chose us in Him before the creation of the world to be holy and blameless in His sight. In love, He predestined us to be adopted as His sons through Jesus Christ, in accordance with His pleasure and will - to the praise of His glorious grace, which He has freely given us in the One He loves."

Ephesians 1:11-12 "In Him we were also chosen, having been predestined according to the plan of Him who works out everything in conformity with the purpose of His will, in order that we, who were the first to hope in Christ, might be for the praise of His glory."

We were chosen by His grace, not by our works, to receive His grace and the gift of His salvation.

Romans 11:5-6 "So too, at the present time there is a remnant chosen by grace. And if by grace, then it is no longer by works; if it were, grace would no longer be grace."

If the Lord has a calling on your life you will only be able to run so far before He calls on you to "come forth." God's purpose will prevail.

Isaiah 46:10 "I say: My purpose will stand, and I will do all that I please."

Just like Moses, Peter, Paul, and Mary if God has a calling on your life, the chain of events and people in your life will take place. God's purpose will prevail, and nothing can thwart God's plans.

Job 42:2 "I know that You can do all things; no plan of Yours can be thwarted."

Romans 8:29-30 "For those God foreknew He also predestined to be conformed to the likeness of His Son, that He might be the firstborn among many brothers. And those He predestined, He also called; those He called, He also justified; those He justified, He also glorified."

God will call out your name as He did with Lazarus.

Hebrews 9:15 "For this reason Christ is the mediator of a new covenant, that those who are called may receive the promised eternal inheritance - now that He has died as a ransom to set them free from the sins committed under the first covenant."

There will be events that will happen that will aid in leading you to salvation.

Job 33:29-30 "God does all these things to a man - twice, even three times - to turn back his soul from the pit, that the Light of life may shine on him."

God knows your heart and lets these things happen to you to call you out of darkness.

1 Peter 2:9 "But you are a chosen people, a royal priesthood, a holy nation, a people belonging to God, that you may declare the praises of Him who called you out of darkness into His wonderful light."

Not only will God use events but He will also use people.

Matthew 9:38 "Ask the Lord of the harvest, therefore, to send out workers into His harvest field."

God also knows your heart and even better than you know it yourself.

Proverbs 19:21 "Many are the plans in a man's heart, but it is the Lord's purpose that prevails."

Psalm 139:1 "O Lord, you have searched me and you know me."

Then when you finally come to the end of yourself, when things look the worse that they could be and utterly hopeless, that is when you will call on God and He will be there.

Jeremiah 29:12-14 "Then you will call upon Me and come and pray to Me, and I will listen to you. You will seek Me and find Me when you seek Me with all your heart. I will be found by you, declares the Lord, and bring you back from captivity."

You have to open the door but God knows your heart and He knows that knock at the door that will bring you to your knees in repentance and open the door and let Him in.

Revelation 3:20 "Here I am! I stand at the door and knock. If anyone hears my voice and opens the door, I will come in and eat with him, and he with Me."

That last knock at the door, that event that God has planned will be the one when things look so hopeless that there is no other way out. That is when God will call out your name.

Isaiah 55:11-12 "So is My Word that goes out from My mouth: It will not return to Me empty but will accomplish what I desire and achieve the purpose for which I sent it. You will go out in joy and be led forth in peace."

At God's calling He will open your eyes so that you will have spiritual eyes to see, spiritual ears to hear, and a spiritual heart to understand and be set free.

Isaiah 42:6-7 "I, the Lord, have called you in righteousness; I will take hold of your hand. I will keep you and will make you to be a covenant for the people and a light for the Gentiles, to open eyes that are blind, to free captives from prison, and to release from the dungeon those who sit in darkness."

John 8:32 "Then you will know the truth, and the truth will set you free."

As you open the door and invite Jesus into your heart your wounds will be healed, and your sins will be forgiven and the chains of sin that have kept you in bondage with a heavy heart will be loosed.

Ephesians 1:7-8 "In Him we have redemption through His blood, the forgiveness of sins, in accordance with the riches of God's grace that He lavished on us with all wisdom and understanding."

You will be a new person in Christ with a new heart, one that has been set free!

Everyone who has a lost loved one or friend, keep praying. Don't give up.

Luke 18:1 "Then Jesus told His disciples a parable to show them that they should always pray and not give up."

God will save them but in His time. After all, He is God.

Acts 16:31 "Believe in the Lord Jesus, and you will be saved - you and your household."

God already knows the outcome, it is victory! With God, there can be nothing less.

Psalm 60:12 "With God we will gain the victory, and He will trample down our enemies."

Praise the Lord! He will call your lost loved ones just as He did with Lazarus! When God says, "Come forth" they will be loosed! There will be people there that God will use to help lead them. Just trust in God.

Matthew 18:18 "I tell you the truth, whatever you bind on earth will be bound in heaven, and whatever you loose on earth will be loosed in heaven."

Then they will be a child of God. A child of God set free from sin!

John 8:36 "So if the Son sets you free, you will be free indeed."

Jesus Is The Way Where There Is No Way

John 14:6 "I am the Way and the Truth and the Life. No one comes to the Father except through me."

Are you going through turmoil, your world seems to be falling apart and turning upside down. There seems to be no way out of the situation that you are in. You may be a child of God, and this is an enormous trial you are going through. Maybe you believe in Jesus, in God as Creator but you have never given Him complete control of your life, heart, and soul. You have never repented of your sins. This may be an eye-opener for you. God may be trying to get your attention; it is better to endure excruciating pain on earth through a difficult trial than to suffer an eternity in hell. Eternity is a long, long time. It is forever! In all these situations, look to Jesus. **Jesus is the way when there is no way.**

Job 33:29-30 "God does all these things to a man - twice, even three times - to turn back his soul from the pit that the light of life may shine on him."

2 Peter 3:9 "He is patient with you, not wanting anyone to perish, but everyone to come to repentance."

1 Thessalonians 5:9-10 "For God did not appoint us to suffer wrath but to receive salvation through our Lord Jesus Christ. He died for us so that, whether we are awake or asleep, we may live together with Him."

If the latter pertains to you, then the answer is simple. *Repent!* Give your will, heart, and soul to God! Ask for forgiveness of your sins and ask Jesus to come into your heart. Then your trial will turn around and disappear and all your sins will be forgiven and forgotten! Completely erased! A brand-new start! How awesome!

Psalm 37:37-40 "Consider the blameless, observe the upright; there is a future for the man of peace. But all the sinners will be destroyed; the future of the wicked will be cut off. The salvation of the righteous comes from the Lord; He is their stronghold in times of trouble. The Lord helps them and delivers them; He delivers them from the wicked and saves them because they take refuge in Him."

Romans 10:9-10 "That if you confess with your mouth, 'Jesus is Lord,' and believe in your heart that God raised Him from the dead, you will be saved. For it is with your heart that you believe and are justified, and it is with your mouth that you confess and are saved."

James 4:10 "Humble yourselves before the Lord, and He will lift you up."

Hebrews 8:12 "For I will forgive their wickedness and will remember their sins no more."

He will not knock on the door of your heart forever! Do not take the chance of procrastinating and thinking that you have forever. You will procrastinate yourself straight into hell! Your trials and sorrows will increase, and death may be at your doorstep. Then it is too late! Only God knows the hour and time of your death. If you do not repent, eternity in hell is your own choice.

Revelation 3:20 "Here I am! I stand at the door and knock. If anyone hears My voice and opens the door, I will come in and eat with him and he with Me."

Matthew 7:21-23 "Not everyone who says to Me, 'Lord, Lord,' will enter the kingdom of heaven, but only he who does the will of My Father who is in heaven. Many will say to Me on that day, 'Lord, Lord, did we not prophesy in Your name, and in Your name drive out demons and perform many miracles?' Then I will tell them plainly, 'I never knew you. Away from Me, you evildoers!"

Isaiah 55:6-7 "Seek the Lord while He may be found; call on Him while He is near. Let the wicked forsake his way and the evil man his thoughts. Let him turn to the Lord, and He will have mercy on him, and to God, for He will freely pardon."

This verse says, "Seek the Lord while He may be found." This means that He will not knock on the door of your heart forever. He will not always be found. So in your overwhelming trial, you feel the conviction of the Holy Spirit, answer the call before it is too late!

John 15:8 "When He comes, He will convict the world of guilt in regard to sin and righteousness and judgment."

Job 14:5 "Man's days are determined; you have decreed the number of his months and have set limits he cannot exceed."

Psalm 16:4 "The sorrows of those will increase who run after other gods."

Obadiah: 15 "The day of the Lord is near for all nations. As you have done, it will be done to you; your deeds will return upon your own head."

Jonah 2:8 "Those who cling to worthless idols forfeit the grace that could be theirs."

Jeremiah 2:19 "Your wickedness will punish you; your backsliding will rebuke you."

Jeremiah 4:18 "Your own conduct and actions have brought this upon you. This is your punishment. How bitter it is! How it pierces to the heart!"

We are not greater than God. He is God Almighty! Creator of heaven earth and all that is in it. All belongs to God. He is Sovereign overall. We cannot keep doing our own will and living according to our sinful nature and expect to die and go to heaven. Would you let your child talk back to you, disobey you, and show you complete disregard and no respect at all and still let them ask for rewards? Would you not punish them? Well God is our heavenly Father and He punishes as well. Where you go when you leave this world is your choice!

Psalm 24:1-2 "The earth is the Lord's, and everything in it, the world, and all who live in it; for He founded it upon the seas and established it upon the waters."

John 13:15-17 "I have set you an example that you should do as I have done for you. I tell you the truth, no servant is greater than his master, nor is a messenger greater than the one who sent him. Now that you know these things, you will be blessed if you do them."

Galatians 5:19-21 "The acts of the sinful nature are obvious: sexual immorality, impurity, and debauchery; idolatry and witchcraft; hatred, discord, jealousy, fits of rage, selfish ambition, dissensions, factions, and envy; drunkenness, orgies, and the like. I warn you, as I did before, that those who live like this will not inherit the kingdom of God."

1 Corinthians 10:21-22 "You cannot drink the cup of the Lord and the cup of demons too; you cannot have a part in both the Lord's table and the table of demons. Are we trying to arouse the Lord's jealousy? Are we stronger than He?"

To the child of God going through overwhelming trials

When we receive Jesus Christ into our hearts we are born again. We will have the understanding of Jesus Christ, with His Spirit within us. As you read the Word of God you will understand it and as you grow as a Christian, more and more of the Bible will make sense to you. You learn in school little by little, well so it is with your Christian walk.

One thing you need to understand, just because you are now a Christian, it does not mean that you are all of a sudden the perfect Christian. That is a day-by-day process that can only be learned through trials. Someone can tell you how to do something, but until you do it a few times, do you know it? Just telling you, you can forget. Learning through trials, it becomes part of you. As a child, we learn through our mistakes and the discipline of our parents, right from wrong. After a few punishments, we learn to do right. It becomes a part of who we are and how we act. So it is with our Christian walk. Our trials mold us into who God wants us to be. What God is trying to teach us can only be interwoven into our spirits through trials.

Ezekiel 36:26 "I will give you a new heart and put a new spirit in you; I will remove from you your heart of stone and give you a heart of flesh."

2 Corinthians 5:17 "Therefore, if anyone is in Christ, he is a new creation; the old has gone, the new has come!"

Galatians 2:20 "The life I live in the body, I live by faith in the Son of God, who loved me and gave Himself for me."

Galatians 4:6-7 "Because you are sons, God sent the Spirit of His Son into our hearts, the Spirit who calls out, "*Abba*, Father.' So you are no longer a slave, but a son; and since you are a son, God has made you also an heir."

The Spirit of Jesus lives within us when we are born again. We have a new understanding of the Bible as we read it and a new-found desire to read it. But we have years of the world in us that God can only clean out little by little, day by day, trial by trial.

Deuteronomy 7:22 "The Lord your God will drive out those nations before you, little by little. You will not be allowed to eliminate them all at once, or the wild animals will multiply around you."

1 Thessalonians 5:23 "May God Himself, the God of all peace, sanctify you through and through."

James 1:2-5 "Consider it pure joy, my brothers, whenever you face trials of many kinds because you know that the testing of your faith develops perseverance. Perseverance must finish its work so that you may be mature and complete, not lacking anything. If any of you lacks wisdom, he should ask God, who gives generously to all without finding fault, and it will be given to him."

1 Peter 1:6-7 "In this you greatly rejoice, though now for a little while you may have had to suffer grief in all kinds of trials. These have come so that your faith - of greater worth than gold, which perishes even though refined by fire - may be proved genuine and may result in praise, glory, and honor when Jesus Christ is revealed."

1 Peter 2:20-24 "But if you suffer for doing well and you endure it, this is commendable before God. To this you were called, because Christ suffered for you, leaving you an example that you should follow in His steps. 'He committed no sin, and no deceit was found in His mouth.' When they hurled their insults at Him, He did not retaliate; when He suffered, He made no threats. Instead, He entrusted Himself to Him who judges justly. He Himself for our sins in His body on the tree, so that we might die to sins and live for righteousness; by His wounds you have been healed."

1 Peter 4:16 "However, if you suffer as a Christian, do not be ashamed, but praise God that you bear that name."

Romans 8:17-18 "Now if we are children, then we are heirs of God and co-heirs with Christ, if indeed we share in His sufferings in order that we may also share in His glory. I consider that our present sufferings are not worth comparing with the glory that will be revealed in us."

It is better to suffer as a Christian and know that your eternal home is in heaven. Christ suffered, are we better than He that we should be exempt from it? He was sinless; we are not. To know that as a child of God, your help is in Jesus Christ and when you have learned what it is that He is trying to teach you, He will lift you up should give you hope. But if you are not a Christian and you are suffering, until you repent and receive Jesus, you are hopeless.

1 Peter 5:8-11 "Be self-controlled and alert. Your enemy the devil prowls around like a roaring lion looking for someone to devour. Resist him, standing firm in the faith, because you know that your brothers throughout the world are undergoing the same kind of suffering. And the God of all grace, who called you to His eternal glory in Christ, after you have suffered a little while, will Himself restore you and make you strong, firm, and steadfast. To Him be the power forever and ever. Amen."

If you are feeling overwhelmed and keep getting sidetracked by the circumstances and just cannot seem to keep your eyes on Jesus, just call on His name and He will pick you up. When Peter saw Jesus walking on the water He got out of the boat and started toward Him. As long as he kept his eyes on Jesus, he walked on water. You can too. Through Jesus alone, the impossible is made possible. When he took his eyes off Jesus and looked at his circumstances he started to fall. You will too. But Jesus was quick to pick him up and he will pick you up as well. He is faithful to all His promises. Stand on His Word. Every promise will be fulfilled.

Psalm 145:13-14 "The Lord is faithful to all His promises and loving to all He has made. The Lord upholds all those who fall and lifts up all who are bowed down."

Proverbs 18:10 "The name of the Lord is a strong tower; the righteous run to it and are safe."

Joshua 21:43-45 "So the Lord gave Israel all the land He had sworn to give their forefathers, and they took possession of it and settled there. The Lord gave them rest on every side, just as He had sworn to their forefathers. Not one of their enemies withstood them; the Lord handed all their enemies over to them. Not one of all the Lord's good promises to the house of Israel failed; every one was fulfilled."

Hebrews 12:2-3 "Let us fix our eyes on Jesus, the author, and perfecter of our faith, who for the joy set before Him endured the cross, scorning its shame, and sat down at the right hand of the throne of God. Consider Him who endured such opposition from sinful men, so that you will not grow weary and lose heart."

Psalm 138:2 "For you have exalted above all things Your Name and Your Word."

Matthew 19:26 "With man this is impossible, but with God, all things are possible."

Look to Jesus for your strength. Look to Him to help you in trouble and strengthen your faith. He loves you and will never leave you nor forsake you. Stay in the Word. It is your strength to fight off Satan, without Jesus and His Word you are helpless. Ask God to help you get through your trial and to show you the way. He will come to your rescue and answer your prayer.

Deuteronomy 31:6 "Be strong and courageous. Do not be afraid or terrified because of them, for the Lord your God goes with you; he will never leave you nor forsake you."

John 15:5 "I am the vine; you are the branches. If a man remains in Me and I in him, he will bear much fruit; apart from Me you can do nothing."

John 6:47-48 "I tell you the truth, he who believes has everlasting life. I am the bread of life."

Psalm 25:3-5 "No one whose hope is in you will ever be put to shame, but they will be put to shame who are treacherous without excuse. Show me your ways, O Lord, teach me your paths; guide me in your truth and teach me, for you are God my Savior, and my hope is in you all day long."

Psalm 29:11 "The Lord gives strength to His people; the Lord blesses His people with peace."

Psalm 32:7 "You are my hiding place; you will protect me from trouble."

Psalm 34:4 "I sought the Lord, and He answered me; He delivered me from all my fears."

Psalm 34:17-19 "The righteous cry out, and the Lord hears them; He delivers them from all their troubles. The Lord is close to the brokenhearted and saves those who are crushed in spirit. A righteous man may have many troubles, but the Lord delivers him from them all."

Psalm 46:1 "God is our refuge and strength, an ever-present help in trouble."

Psalm 46:10 "Be still and know that I am God."

Psalm 55:22 "Cast your cares on the Lord and He will sustain you; He will never let the righteous fall."

Psalm 56:4 "In God, whose Word I praise, in God I trust; I will not be afraid. What can mortal man do to me?"

Philippians 4:13 "I can do everything through Him who gives me strength."

He already knows the outcome! He has been through ahead of you. You are assured of the outcome. You win! Knowing that He has already been through your trial ahead of you should help you to remember that victory is yours. Just don't give up. Victory is only ours through Jesus Christ.   He is our victory and our strength. The end of your trial will come. Keep trusting in Jesus. Only He will lead you through to victory!

Deuteronomy 9:3 "But be assured today that the Lord your God is the one who goes across ahead of you like a devouring fire. He will destroy them; He will subdue them before you. And you will drive them out and annihilate them quickly, as the Lord has promised."

Proverbs 3:5-6 "Trust in the Lord with all your heart and lean not on your own understanding; in all your ways acknowledge Him, and He will make your paths straight."

Ecclesiastes 3:1 "There is a time for everything and a season for every activity under heaven."

Ecclesiastes 8:6 "For there is a proper time and procedure for every matter, though a man's misery weighs heavily upon him."

Jeremiah 29:11 "For I know the plans I have for you,' declares the Lord, 'plans to prosper you and not to harm you, plans to give you hope and a future."

Psalm 33:10-11 "The Lord foils the plans of the nations; He thwarts the purposes of the peoples. But the plans of the Lord stand firm forever, the purposes of His heart through all generations."

1 Corinthians 15:54-58 "Death has been swallowed up in victory. Where, O death, is your victory? Where, O death, is your sting? The sting of death is sin, and the power of sin is the law. But thanks be to God! He gives us the victory through our Lord Jesus Christ. Therefore, my dear brothers, stand firm. Let nothing move you. Always give yourselves fully to the work of the Lord, because you know that your labor in the Lord is not in vain."

Psalm 60:12 "With God we will gain the victory, and He will trample down our enemies."

A Victorious Walk

To have a victorious walk there are certain things you must do.

Be a child of God

John 1:12 "Yet to all who received Him, to those who believe in His name, He gave the right   to become children of God."

To be a true child of God, you need to make Jesus the Lord of your life and be devoted to doing His will.

Matthew 7:21 "Not everyone who says to me, 'Lord, Lord,' will enter the kingdom of heaven, but only he who does the will of My Father who is in heaven."

Through this and by your faith in Him you are saved and are now a child of God.

Romans 3:23-25 "For all have sinned and fall short of the glory of God, and are justified freely by His grace through the redemption that came by Christ Jesus. God presented Him as a sacrifice of atonement, through faith in His blood."

Romans 10:10 "For it is with your heart that you believe and are justified, and it is with your mouth that you confess and are saved."

Be devoted to God

Because of God, who He is, and what he did for us, we have an escape from hell: eternal death.

Romans 5:8 "But God demonstrated His love for us in this: While we were still sinners, Christ died for us."

Romans 6:23 "For the wages of sin is death, but the gift of God is eternal life in Christ Jesus our Lord."

Matthew 22:37-38 "Love the Lord your God with all your heart and with all your soul and with all your mind. This is the first and greatest commandment."

We must be obedient to the will of God. Walk in all his ways.

Joshua 22:5 "But be very careful to keep the commandment and the law of Moses the servant of the Lord gave you: to love the Lord your God, to walk in all His ways, to obey His commands, to hold fast to Him and to serve Him with all your heart and all your soul."

Be strong and courageous, not fearful.

Deuteronomy 20:2-4 "Hear, O Israel, today you are going into battle against your enemies. Do not be fainthearted or afraid; do not be terrified or give way to panic before them. For the Lord your God is the One who goes with you to fight for you against your enemies to give you victory."

Meditate on the Word of God

The Word is your spiritual strength.

Joshua 1:8-9 "Do not let the Book of the Law depart from your mouth; meditate on it day and night, so that you may be careful to do everything written in it. Then you will be prosperous and successful. Have I not commanded you? Be strong and courageous. Do not be terrified; do not be discouraged, for the Lord your God will be with you wherever you go."

It is your "bread of life" that gives you strength to endure and overcome your trials.

John 6:35 "I am the bread of life. He who comes to me will never go hungry, and he who believes in me will never be thirsty. But as I told you, you have seen me and still you do not believe. All that the Father gives me will come to me, and whoever comes to me I will never drive away. For I have come down from heaven not to do My will but to do the will of Him who sent Me. And this is the will of Him who sent Me, that I shall lose nothing of all that He has given Me but raise them up at the last day."

Philippians 4:13 "I can do everything through Him who gives me strength."

Jesus Himself endured. He suffered and was humiliated, ridiculed, beaten, and crucified. He still walked in love and even to the end, He died with love.

Luke 23:34 "Father, forgive them, for they do not know what they are doing."

He set the example for us to follow.

John 13:15 "I have set you an example that you should do as I have done for you."

Reading the Word of God will guide you in all truth.

John 8:31-32 "If you hold to my teaching, you are really my disciples. Then you will know the truth, and the truth will set you free."

We learn and grow as we overcome our trials and meditate on the Word of God. This helps us to live a life of freedom.

John 8:36 "So if the Son sets you free, you will be free indeed."

In Jesus Christ only will you have victory!

1 Corinthians 15:54-58 "Death has been swallowed up in victory. Where, O death, is your victory? Where, O death, is your sting? The sting of death is sin, and the power of sin is the law. But thanks be to God! He gives us the victory through our Lord Jesus Christ. Therefore, my dear brothers, stand firm. Let nothing move you. Always give yourselves fully to the work of the Lord, because you know that your labor in the Lord is not in vain."

Love God, speak in love, act in love; walk in all of love's ways, and be thankful and praise God always. In doing this you will have a victorious, Christian Walk.

CHAPTER 2

Beginning Your Walk: Fighting The Flesh

In this chapter, you will read Bible studies dealing with the flesh. Your flesh will get you into all sorts of trouble if you let it. "Watch and pray so that you will not fall into temptation. "The spirit is willing, but the body is weak," (Mark 14:38). The flesh is temptation's breeding ground if your heart and mind are not set on obeying God and loving Him, and doing what pleases Him. The flesh is weak, and we need to be strong in the Lord in order to overcome it.

"So, if you think you are standing firm, be careful that you don't fall! No temptation has seized you except what is common to man. And God is faithful; He will not let you be tempted beyond what you can bear. But when you are tempted, He will also provide a way out so that you can stand up under it," (1 Corinthians 10:12-13).

The fruit of the Spirit will grow within you with each lesson the Lord teaches you through the trials of life. One aspect of the fruit of the Spirit is self-control, which is truly needed in order to overcome the temptations of the flesh or carnal nature and the attacks the devil sends your way. "But the fruit of the Spirit is love, joy, peace, patience, kindness, goodness, faithfulness, gentleness and self-control," (Galatians 5:22-23).

Through the trials of life impurities are weeded out and the fruit of the Spirit grows more and more.

"He replied, "Every plant that my heavenly Father has not planted will be pulled up by the roots," (Matthew 15:13).

Are You Carnally Or Spiritually Minded?

Romans 8:5-9 "Those who live according to the sinful nature have their minds set on what that nature desires, but those who live in accordance with the Spirit have their minds set on what the Spirit desires. The mind of sinful man is death, but the mind controlled by the Spirit is life and peace; the sinful mind is hostile to God. It does not submit to God's law, nor can it do so. Those controlled by the sinful nature cannot please God. You, however, are controlled not by the sinful nature but by the Spirit, if the Spirit of God lives in you."

Trouble and hardships come to everyone as long as we live here on earth. In the beginning, when God created us He gave us free will, and sometimes hardships come because of it; people, including ourselves, do not always make the right choices and we "reap what we sow" because of it or we become a part of someone else's consequences. But take heart, our heavenly Father is a God of love, and He will not let us go through anything unless we can learn something out of it or it can draw something out of us that does not need to be there. The death and resurrection of Jesus Christ who died for our sins is proof enough of the love of God.

Matthew 15:13 "Every plant that my heavenly Father has not planted will be pulled up by the roots."

Do you rely on other people or your job to supply your needs? Is your joy dependent on your current situation? Are you constantly dwelling on the "what about me's," your feelings, hurts, and needs and if others would do right or the right job would come along then you would be happy? If you can answer truthfully "yes" to these questions, then you are carnally minded or living according to the sinful nature. To live spiritually mind is to live by faith. God will use other people or our jobs to supply our needs, but they are not the supplier. Our supplication and our joy come from God.

Romans 1:17 "For in the gospel a righteousness from God is revealed, a righteousness that is by faith from first to last, just as it is written: "The righteous will live by faith."

As children of God, we know that our faith, hope, strength, love, and physical and emotional needs are all supplied by God. In knowing this we have joy in our hearts. Joy in knowing that no matter what we go through our needs will be supplied.

Philippians 4:11-13 "I am not saying this because I am in need, for I have learned to be content whatever the circumstances. I know what it is to be in need, and I know what it is to have plenty. I have learned the secret of being content in any and every situation, whether well-fed or hungry, whether living in plenty or in want. I can do everything through him who gives me strength."

Philippians 4:19 "And my God will meet all your needs according to His glorious riches in Christ Jesus."

Genesis 22:14 "And Abraham called the name of that place Jehovah Jireh: as it is said to this day, in the mount of the Lord it shall be seen."

God provides for our spiritual needs, our salvation, faith, hope, and peace.

Salvation

Acts 4:12 "Salvation is found in no one else, for there is no other name under heaven given to men by which we must be saved."

Love

John 4:7-12 "Dear friends, let us love one another, for love comes from God. Everyone who loves has been born of God and knows God. Whoever does not love does not know God, because God is love. This is how God showed His love among us: He sent His one and only Son into the world so that we might live through Him. This is love: not that we loved God, but that He loved us and sent His Son as an atoning sacrifice for our sins. Dear friends, since God so loved us, we also ought to love one another. No one has ever seen God; but if we love one another, God lives in us, and His love is made complete in us."

Romans 5:5 "And hope does not disappoint us, because God has poured out His love into our hearts by the Holy Spirit, whom he has given us."

Faith

Hebrews 12:2-3 "Let us fix our eyes on Jesus, the author, and perfecter of our faith, who for the joy set before Him endured the cross, scorning its shame, and sat down at the right hand of the throne of God. Consider Him who endured such opposition from sinful men, so that you will not grow weary and lose heart."

Luke 17:5 "The apostles said to the Lord, "Increase our faith!"

Peace

John 14:27 "Peace I leave with you; my peace I give you. I do not give to you as the world gives. Do not let your hearts be troubled and do not be afraid."

Strength

Psalm 29:11 "The Lord gives strength to His people; the Lord blesses His people with peace."

Joy

Luke 1:14) "He will be a joy and delight to you, and many will rejoice because of His birth."

Hope

Romans 15:13) "May the God of hope fill you with all joy and peace as you trust in Him, so that you may overflow with hope by the power of the Holy Spirit."

1 Peter 1:3-5 "Praise be to the God and Father of our Lord Jesus Christ! In His great mercy, he has given us new birth into a living hope through the resurrection of Jesus Christ from the dead, and into an inheritance that can never perish, spoil, or fade—kept in heaven for you, who through faith are shielded by God's power until the coming of the salvation that is ready to be revealed in the last time."

God provides for our physical needs, which are our healing, food, money for housing and clothes, and emotional needs which are a sound mind and happiness.

Healing

1 Peter 2:24 "He Himself bore our sins in His body on the tree, so that we might die to sins and live for righteousness; by His wounds you have been healed."

Nourishment

Matthew 6:31-34 "So do not worry, saying, 'What shall we eat?' or 'What shall we drink?' or 'What shall we wear?' For the pagans run after all these things, and your heavenly Father knows that you need them. But seek first His kingdom and His righteousness, and all these things will be given to you as well. Therefore, do not worry about tomorrow, for tomorrow will worry about itself. Each day has enough trouble of its own."

Psalm 147:14 "He grants peace to your borders and satisfies you with the finest of wheat."

Happiness

Isaiah 51:11 "The ransomed of the Lord will return. They will enter Zion with singing; everlasting joy will crown their heads. Gladness and joy will overtake them, and sorrow and sighing will flee away."

Sound mind

2 Timothy 1:7 "For God hath not given us the spirit of fear; but of power, and of love, and of a sound mind."

How do you live spiritually minded in a world where not everyone is a Christian and believes in "do unto others" and "love your neighbor as yourself?"

1. Read the Word- Faith comes by hearing.

Romans 10:17 "Consequently, faith comes from hearing the message, and the message is heard through the word of Christ."

Romans 12:2 "Do not conform any longer to the pattern of this world but be transformed by the renewing of your mind. Then you will be able to test and approve what God's will is—His good, pleasing, and perfect will."

2. Cast Down - Trash those depressing thoughts!

2 Corinthians 10:4-5 "The weapons we fight with are not the weapons of the world. On the contrary, they have divine power to demolish strongholds. We demolish arguments and every pretension that sets itself up against the knowledge of God, and we take captive every thought to make it obedient to Christ."

3. Confess the Word and speak it! - Write down Scriptures about your situation, pray it, and speak it out!

2 Corinthians 4:13-15 "It is written: "I believed; therefore, I have spoken." With that same spirit of faith, we also believe and therefore speak, because we know that the one who raised the Lord Jesus from the dead will also raise us with Jesus and present us with you in his presence. All this is for your benefit, so that the grace that is reaching more and more people may cause thanksgiving to overflow to the glory of God."

Psalm 138:2 "I will bow down toward your holy temple and will praise Your Name for your love and your faithfulness, for you have exalted above all things Your Name and your Word."

Proverbs 18:21 "The tongue has the power of life and death, and those who love it will eat its fruit."

Romans 10: 10 "For it is with your heart that you believe and are justified, and it is with your mouth that you confess and are saved."

Romans 4:17 "As it is written: "I have made you a father of many nations." He is our father in the sight of God, in whom he believed—the God who gives life to the dead and calls things that are not as though they were."

4. Pray Continuously - Talk to God! He is your Friend, your Father, your Creator, your Savior, your Peace, your Life, your Counselor, and your Deliverer, etc.

Luke 18:1 "Then Jesus told His disciples a parable to show them that they should always pray and not give up."

1 Thessalonians 5:16-18 "Be joyful always; pray continually; give thanks in all circumstances, for this is God's will for you in Christ Jesus."

Emotional Distress

Do not base what you do on Emotions. Bad emotions include but are not restricted to:

1. Anger
2. Irritability
3. Depression, anxiety
4. Sadness
5. Blasé - not wanting to do anything laziness (lacking self-control) is a big no-no!

Psalm 4:4, Proverbs 6:6-19; 14:29; 26:13-16; 25:28

These emotions cause you to sin if you give in to them. Yes, we must trust God, but that does not mean taking Him for granted and expecting Him to do everything for us and provide everything for us while we sit back and do nothing when we are quite capable of getting our hands dirty (2 Kings 17:1-9).

Many times, when we get depressed or overwhelmed by attacks from the enemy; we do not feel like reading the Bible. It just seems to take away all our energy, drive, and hope. This is when we need to read the Bible anyway knowing that once we get into it, we will realize that the worst part of doing what it is that we try to get out of is getting started. For Christ is our strength and our joy. Drawing near to Him will bring your joy back.

Nehemiah 8:10 "For the joy of the Lord is your strength."

Philippians 4:13 "I can do everything through Him who gives me strength."

James 4:8 "Come near to God and He will come near to you."

After we start to get our hands dirty, then we should be too busy with the task at hand to let Satan worm his way into our minds giving us thoughts of complaint.

I have experienced this myself. As soon as I started to read the depression seemed to just slip away. The Lord says, "I am the Lord, who heals you," (Exodus 15:26). This is everything from our spiritual needs to our physical and emotional needs as well. The Bible is our strength, and it is the only way that we can defend ourselves against the onslaught of Satan's attacks. The forces of darkness attack us with these fits of depression, despair, hopelessness, anger, resentment, or whatever other emotion that you let consume you (including the 5 listed above) starting with the minutest whisper that worms its way into your serenity. Before long, you start to acknowledge that the whisper is there instead of shrugging it off out of faith or with a Bible verse, which relates to the matter. At that time the demon's little whisper becomes your thought and in turn, you begin to argue with it, which causes doubt and fear to creep in unawares. Then before you know it, half the day has gone by and what was once a gnat has grown into a bee-sting that could take a few days of torment to heal. Why do you think it is in these times that it is the hardest to pick up the Bible and read -- because IT IS DURING THESE TIMES THAT YOU NEED THE WORD OF GOD THE MOST!!!

At this point, when the emotions already have a foothold on you, the only way to get rid of them is to go to God in prayer and worship Him. Then reading the Bible will "let the dogs loose" so to speak and if you do not feel better right away, then have faith while in your depression and worship God anyway. After all, *anyone* can praise God in times of joy, but God wants His children to praise Him always. Why? Because He is God, and we need no other reason which He makes clear in the Book of Job. Do you not have anything to praise Him for in your sadness?

Philippians 3:8 "Yet indeed I also count all things loss for the excellence of the knowledge of Christ Jesus my Lord, for whom I have suffered the loss of all things, and count them as rubbish, that I may gain Christ."

Romans 8:18-19 "For I consider that the sufferings of this present time are not worthy to be compared with the glory which shall be revealed in us. For the earnest expectation of the creation eagerly waits for the revealing of the sons of God."

That last part, "Sons of God" includes you, and so you can also state your life on this.

Romans 8:35-39 "Who shall separate us from the love of Christ? Shall tribulation, or distress, or persecution, or famine, or nakedness, or peril, or sword? As it is written: 'For your sake, we are killed all day long; we are accounted as sheep for the slaughter.' Yet in all these things we are more than conquerors through Him who loved us. For I am persuaded that neither death nor life, nor angels nor principalities nor powers, nor things present nor things to come, nor height nor depth, nor any other created thing, shall be able to separate us from the love of God which is in Christ Jesus our Lord."

Amen, Hallelujah! Glory and honor to El Shaddai the ALMIGHTY GOD!

If the above verses do not make your spirit sing to Him, then you need to read them again and give them to Him in praise. The result just might be earth-shaking!! Crucify these emotions of the flesh. If you disregard this good advice and keep letting these emotions rule you- God will discipline you or let your distress, send you into hopelessness until you come to Him and repent or spill your heart to Him in ALL honesty.

Galatians 5:24-25 "Those who belong to Christ Jesus have crucified the sinful nature with its passions and desires. Since we live by the Spirit, let us keep in step with the Spirit."

Galatians 5:16 "So, I say, live by the Spirit and you will not gratify the desires of the sinful nature."

By not reading the Word, the very thing that could restore the fruits of the Spirit which include "...love, joy peace, patience, kindness, goodness, faithfulness, gentleness, and self-control," (Galatians 5:22-23). By not reading the Word you are gratifying the desires of the flesh. What is that? How are you gratifying them?

Take these two things into account:

1. You do not read the Bible because you have that unfaithful thought "It will not help me to read."

2. You do not feel like it because you are lazy

Proverbs 6:9-11 "How long will you slumber, O sluggard? When will you rise from your sleep? A little sleep, a little slumber, A little folding of the hands to sleep - So shall your poverty come on you like a prowler, and your need like an armed man."

Ecclesiastes 10:18 "Because of laziness the building decays, and through idleness of hands the house leaks."

God is ordering you to feel better because if you do not, it will make Him feel bad. In the Bible, He wept bitterly at the rebellion of the Israelites. God wants you to have joy and he wants to bless you (John 10:10). When you rebel against him, he weeps (Jeremiah 13:15-17). Wow! Considering these things, you are either unfaithful which does not please God, or you are lazy, in which God condemns in the second point. Does it make you feel good to have to apply either one to your case if indeed it does? Well, do not be discouraged because the first step is identifying the problem and believing you messed up. The second is taking it to God in all humility and without any excuses or justification!! God is holy and by trying to justify your sin you are destroying the humility and repentance you came into His presence in that His Holiness demands.

Worldly sorrow is being sorry to the point that you regret being caught whether you realize this or not. 2 Corinthians 7:10 says "Godly sorrow brings repentance that leads to salvation and leaves no regret, but worldly sorrow brings death." Do you want to go to hell? I thought not, so quit trying to justify and make excuses for your sin; get rid of your pride (saying "God, we are both right because I had an excuse to sin, but you have the right to punish me") and humble yourself before God and repent. Admitting your sins is the only way to grow. Maturing as a Christian and pleasing our Heavenly Father is what He wants of us.

Another part of growing as a Christian is being self-controlled. That is part of the fruit of the Spirit. Being self-controlled is being self-disciplined. I don't know about you, but I would rather watch myself and correct my own mistakes and sins I commit than wait for God to do it. His way may bring more trials. I for one do not want any more than I have to go through. We have to discipline ourselves to do what is right and not be dependent on anyone as well, whether we *feel* like it or not. When we do this, we will grow and mature as a person and a Christian. Pray always. This keeps you close to God, which keeps Satan away and under your feet where he belongs!

1 Thessalonians 5:16-21 "Be joyful always; pray continually; give thanks in all circumstances, for this is God's will for you in Christ Jesus.

Do not put out the Spirit's fire; do not treat prophecies with contempt. Test everything. Hold on to the good. Avoid every kind of evil."

1 Peter 5:8-9 "Be self-controlled and alert. Your enemy the devil prowls around like a roaring lion looking for someone to devour. Resist him, standing firm in the faith, because you know that your brothers throughout the world are undergoing the same kind of suffering."

2 Corinthians 13:5 "Examine yourselves to see whether you are in the faith; test yourselves."

Psalm 51:10 "Create in me a pure heart, O God, and renew a steadfast spirit within me."

1 Thessalonians 4:11-12 "Make it your ambition to lead a quiet life, to mind your own business and to work with your hands, just as we told you, so that your daily life may win the respect of outsiders and so that you will not be dependent on anybody."

Deuteronomy 6:18 "Do what is right and good in the Lord's sight, so that it may go well with you and you may go in and take over the good land that the Lord promised on oath to your forefathers."

This Promised Land is not only your salvation, but it is the promises and answered prayers God has promised you.

Read Colossians Chapter 3

Therefore, since we are receiving a kingdom that cannot be shaken, let us be thankful, and so worship God acceptably with reverence and awe, for our "God is a consuming fire," (Hebrews 12:28). We need to be thankful to God at all times because even in the discipline it is because He loves us and wants a close relationship with us. "My son do not make light of the Lord's discipline, and do not lose heart when He rebukes you, because the Lord disciplines those he loves, and He punishes everyone He accepts as a son. Endure hardship as discipline; God is treating you as sons," (Hebrews 12:5-7).

Friendship With The World Is Your Downfall!

James 4:4 "You adulterous people, don't you know that friendship with the world is hatred toward God? Anyone who chooses to be a friend of the world becomes an enemy of God.

You do not have to go to hell! It is Your Choice!

Jeremiah 2:19 "Your wickedness will punish you; your backsliding will rebuke you. Consider then and realize how evil and bitter it is for you when you forsake the Lord your God and have no awe of me,' declares the Lord, the Lord Almighty."

You say that you believe in God. That is not enough. James 2:19 below states that. You say that you do not like the hypocrites in the Church and in the world. Well, not reading the Word of God as we are commanded to do and obeying God, doing His will and not our own is rebelling against Him and forsaking Him. His will and His commands are made known in the Bible. If you do not read it you will not know what His will is! Disobeying God's will just because the so-called hypocrites of the world are not a very good reason to go to hell! There is no reason at all when salvation is a gift, free! It is a sign of immaturity! Get over it! Get over your petty offenses, which are destroying your soul alone, and grow up!

Joshua 1:8 "Do not let the Book of the Law depart from your mouth; meditate on it day and night, so that you may be careful to do everything written in it. Then you will be prosperous and successful."

Ezekiel 20:32 "You say, 'We want to be like the nations, like the peoples of the world, who serve wood and stone.'"

The world serves natural things; God is supernatural. God is living and the things of the world are dead.

(Jeremiah 2:27-28) "They say to wood, 'You are my father,' and to stone, 'You gave me birth.' They have turned their backs to me and not their faces; yet when they are in trouble, they say, 'Come and save us!' Where then are the gods, you made for yourselves? Let them come if they can save you when you are in trouble! For you have as many gods as you have towns, O Judah."

The people of the world have many gods such as alcohol, drugs, their self, food, work, sex, TV, video games, or anything else that controls them. The things that they run to for the peace in their heart that they should be getting from the One and only true living God! He is the only One who can give you rest! If you are constantly running to other things to find peace, then those things are your gods, and your eternal home will be hell if you do not repent. Believing is not enough!

James 2:19 "You believe that there is one God. Good! Even the demons believe that - and shudder."

You must admit that you are a sinner and make Jesus the Lord of your whole self, life, heart, and soul and ask Him into your heart with all sincerity. God knows lip service. This is the only way to true salvation, peace, and joy of the Lord. Natural things cannot permanently deliver you. God is supernatural and mighty in power. Natural things are not; they are not living. God is. Consider Jesus who was human. He endured beatings beyond human recognition, humiliation, and the overwhelming pressure of being separated from the Father when He hung on the cross. Not to mention the pain of dying on the cross. So, if He overcame, then only Jesus living in us can help us overcome our worldly problems as well.

1 Corinthians 15:57 "He gives us the victory through our Lord Jesus Christ."

Matthew 11:28 "Come to me all you who are weary and burdened, and I will give you rest."

Acts 4:12 "Salvation is found in no one else, for there is no other name under heaven given to men by which we must be saved."

Isaiah 46:8-10 "Remember this, fix it in mind, take it to heart, you rebels. Remember the former things, those of long ago; I am God, and there is no other; I am God, there is none like me. I make known the end from the beginning, from ancient times, what is still to come. I say: My purpose will stand, and I will do all that I please."

We are not to love the world. It is full of evil and lustful desires, which do not bring about the holiness God desires.

James 1:19-22 "My dear brothers take note of this: Everyone should be quick to listen, slow to speak and slow to become angry, for man's anger does not bring about the righteous life that God desires. Therefore, get rid of all moral filth and the evil that is so prevalent and humbly accept the word planted in you, which can save you."

John 2:15-17 "Do not love the world or anything in the world. If anyone loves the world, the love of the Father is not in him. For everything in the world - the cravings of sinful man, the lust of his eyes, and the boasting of what he has and does - comes not from the Father but from the world. The world and its desires pass away, but the man who does the will of God lives forever."

Friendship with the world is turning your back against God. It is condoning and taking part in worldly pleasures, lusts, and addictions. It is rebelling against God.

James 4:4-6 "You adulterous people, don't you know that friendship with the world is hatred toward God? Anyone who chooses to be a friend of the world becomes an enemy of God. Or do you think Scripture says without reason that the Spirit He caused to live in us envies intensely? But He gives us more grace. That is why Scripture says: 'God opposes the proud but gives grace to the humble."

Colossians 1:21 "Once you were alienated from God and were enemies in your minds because of your evil behavior."

1 Samuel 15:22-23 "To obey is better than sacrifice, and to heed is better than the fat of rams. For rebellion is like the sin of divination, and arrogance is like the evil of idolatry. Because you have rejected the Word of the Lord, He has rejected you as king."

Titus 2:11-12 "For the grace of God that brings salvation has appeared to all men. It teaches us to say "No" to ungodliness and worldly passions, and to live self-controlled, upright, and godly lives in this present age, while we wait for the blessed hope - the glorious appearing of our great God and Savior, Jesus Christ."

Being like the world will be your downfall. Just because the world is partying their selves straight into hell, does that mean that you have to do the same thing? We are in the world, but we are not to be of it.

Mark 8:36 "What good is it for a man to gain the whole world, yet forfeit his soul?"

John 15:19 "If you belonged to the world, it would love you as its own. As it is, you do not belong to the world, but I have chosen you out of the world. That is why the world hates you."

John 17:16 "They are not of the world, even as I am not of it."

We are to be holy. We cannot do this in our own strength. Only in the strength of Jesus Christ and that is done by Him living within our hearts and souls, sanctifying us day by day as we read and put the Word of God into practice.

1 Peter 1:16 "Be holy, because I am holy."

John 16:13 "But when He, the Spirit of truth, comes, He will guide you into all truth."

John 17:17-19 "Sanctify them by the truth; your Word is truth. As you sent me into the world, I have sent them into the world. For them, I sanctify myself, that they too may be truly sanctified."

Hebrews 12:14 "Make every effort to live in peace with all men and to be holy; without holiness no one will see the Lord."

We are to walk in the Spirit drawing our strength to overcome and to live holy, pleasing lives to God through the blood of Jesus Christ who gives us strength. We are to be led by the Spirit.

Philippians 4:13 "I can do everything through Him who gives me strength."

The only way to be led by the Spirit is to read the Word every day and live it. To stay in close contact with God not only by reading the Word but also by praying and talking to Him throughout the day. Start your day and end it by talking to God.

Galatians 5:16-18 "So I say, live by the Spirit, and you will not gratify the desires of the sinful nature. For the sinful nature desires what is contrary to the Spirit, and the Spirit what is contrary to the sinful nature. They are in conflict with each other, so that you do not do what you want. But if you are led by the Spirit, you are not under the law."

To do this you must renew your mind daily with the Word of God. You must stay in the Word.

Romans 12:2 "Do not conform any longer to the pattern of this world but be transformed by the renewing of your mind."

Ephesians 6:13 "Therefore put on the full armor of God, so that when the day of evil comes, you may be able to stand your ground, and after you have done everything, to stand. (Read the rest of Chapter 6 of Ephesians to get the full list of the armor of God.)

The Word is your 'bread,' your strength. The blood of Jesus is your 'living water.'

John 6:35 "I am the bread of life. He who comes to me will never go hungry, and he who believes in me will never be thirsty."

John 6:47-48 "I tell you the truth he who believes has everlasting life. I am the bread of life."

John 7:38 "Whoever believes in me, as the Scripture has said, streams of living water will flow from within him."

The Word of God is life. In reading it and believing it, it is your strength as you hold fast to it and put it into practice.

John 6:63 "The Spirit gives life; the flesh counts for nothing. The words I have spoken to you are spirit and they are life."

Hebrews 4:12 "For the Word of God is living and active. Sharper than any double-edged sword, it penetrates even to dividing soul and spirit, joints and marrow; it judges the thoughts and attitudes of the heart."

Jesus is our salvation. Salvation is found in no one or nothing else; salvation for your soul that you may live eternity in Heaven with Him and not in hell in pure torment forever unending. Jesus is your salvation for the troubles of the world that you have to deal with. In your own strength, there is no hope.

Acts 4:12 "Salvation is found in no one else, for there is no other name under heaven given to men by which we must be saved."

John 8:36 "So if the Son sets you free, you will be free indeed."

John 16:33 "I have told you these things, so that in me you may have peace. In this world, you will have trouble. But take heart! I have overcome the world."

John 11:25-26 "I am the resurrection and the life. He who believes in me will live, even though he dies; and whoever lives and believes in me will never die."

Psalm 34:19 "A righteous man may have many troubles, but the Lord delivers him from them all."

Psalm 31:19 "How great is your goodness, which you have stored up for those who fear you, which you bestow in the sight of men on those who take refuge in you."

Only through Jesus we can be holy and live holy lives, as God desires for us.

Revelation 22:11-12 "Let him who does right continue to do right; and let him who is holy continue to be holy. Behold, I am coming soon! My reward is with me, and I will give to every one according to what he has done. I am the Alpha and the Omega, the First and the Last, the Beginning and the End. Blessed are those who wash their robes, that they may have the right to the tree of life and may go through the gates into the city."

Jesus is the Word that became flesh. All who believe and receive are saved and must be sincere.

John 1:12 "Yet to all who received Him, to those who believed in His name, He gave the right to become children of God."

John 1:14 "The Word became flesh and made His dwelling among us. We have seen His glory, the glory of the One and only, who came from the Father, full of grace and truth."

John 4:24 "God is Spirit, and His worshipers must worship Him in spirit and in truth."

It is only with your heart that you truly submit all (your whole self, heart, soul, mind, emotions, will, and life) to God.

Romans 10:10 "For it is with your heart that you believe and are justified, and it is with your mouth that you confess and are saved."

Those who refuse to Make Jesus the Lord and Savior of their life, who refuse to do the will of God - will perish.

Matthew 7:21 "Not everyone who says to me, 'Lord, Lord,' will enter the kingdom of heaven, but only he who does the will of My Father who is in heaven."

If you ask Jesus into your heart-you must mean it. He knows lip service.

Jeremiah 16:17 "My eyes are on all their ways; they are not hidden from me, nor is their sin concealed from my eyes."

Psalm 44:20-21 "If we had forgotten the name of our God or spread out our hands to a foreign god, would not God have discovered it since He knows the secrets of the heart?"

Psalm 94:11 "The Lord knows the thoughts of man; He knows that they are futile."

Isaiah 29:13 "These people come near to me with their mouth and honor me with their lips, but their hearts are far from me."

Jeremiah 12:2-3 "You are always on their lips but far from their hearts. Yet you know me, O Lord; you see me and test my thoughts about you."

Obadiah: 15 "As you have done, it will be done to you; your deeds will return upon your own head."

Revelation 20:15 "If anyone's name was not found written in the Book of Life, he was thrown into the lake of fire."

Revelation 21:6-8 "He said to me: 'It is done. I am the Alpha and the Omega, the Beginning and the End. To him who is thirsty I will give to drink without cost from the spring of the water of life. He who overcomes will inherit all this, and I will be his God and he will be my son. But the cowardly, the unbelieving, the vile, the murderers, the sexually immoral, those who practice magic arts, the idolaters, and all liars - their place will be in the fiery lake of burning sulfur. This is the second death."

An idol is, according to Webster's New American Dictionary, an image of a god, used as an object of worship or an object of ardent or excessive devotion. According to the words of this dictionary, an idol is something that you worship and anything that you worship is your lord or master.

2 Peter 2:19 "For a man is a slave to whatever has mastered him."

There should be only one who is master over you and that is the Lord your God.

Exodus 20:3 "You shall have no other gods before Me."

What kind of idols do you have in your life? What kind of addictions have mastered you? Are you truly worshiping the Lord your God as you should? If you are not reading His Word as He commands then you will not know what God's will is. Ignorance is not bliss, it is HELL. Being ignorant of what is in the Bible, of what God commands is not an excuse for not doing God's will. Disobedience is disobedience. You will go to hell just as fast whether you are aware of God's will and still do not repent and obey or if you are not aware; because you do not read His Word and are living a sinful, unholy life. If you cannot picture Jesus smoking, doing drugs, getting drunk, committing adultery, or anything else that has taken control of you, become your master, then it is wrong and has become your idol or your god.

Do not believe those who say, "There is no hell." Did they create the heavens and the earth? Did they create all living creatures and all of mankind?

Acts 5:29 "We must obey God rather than men!"

Psalm 56:3-4 "When I am afraid, I will trust in you. In God, whose Word I praise, in God I trust; I will not be afraid. What can mortal man do to me?"

God's Words are true. All Scripture is true and is God's Words breathed into the hearts of the men who wrote it.

Psalm 33:4 "For the Word of the Lord is right and true; He is faithful in all He does."

2 Timothy 3:16 "All Scripture is God breathed."

You will send yourself to hell by rejecting Jesus and the life that you choose to live here on earth.

Isaiah 59:12-13 "For our offenses are many in your sight, and our sins testify against us. Our offenses are ever with us, and we acknowledge our iniquities: rebellion and treachery against the Lord, turning our backs on our God, inciting oppression and revolt, uttering lies our hearts have conceived. So, justice is driven back, and righteousness stands at a distance; truth has stumbled in the streets, honesty cannot enter."

Jeremiah 4:18 "Your own conduct and actions have brought this upon you. This is your punishment. How bitter it is! How it pierces the heart!"

Hosea 14:1 "Return, O Israel, to the Lord your God. Your sins have been your downfall! God does not want you to perish!"

Jeremiah 13:17 "I will weep in secret because of your pride; my eyes will weep bitterly, overflowing with tears, because the Lord's flock will be taken captive."

God does not want robots. That is why He gives us free will. Only a heart that loves out of a choice to do so loves with sincerity and faithfulness. That is the love that God wants from us. That is why He gives us a choice.

If you choose to rebel against God and live an unholy, wicked, evil, lustful life on earth without repentance or ever accepting Jesus as Lord and Savior, who died on the cross; enduring the beatings and pain and scorn, for you me, and the whole world when He was blameless and sinless, then it is your choice to go to hell. Not God's. Romans 10:9-10 says that it is with our mouth that we confess; ours not God's. We must ask Jesus into our hearts. We must come. He already did easy with the Israelites as He parted the Red Sea; rained down manna from heaven and caused water to come from a rock when they were parched with thirst in the desert, yet they still turned away from Him time after time.

Romans 10:9-10 "That if you confess with your mouth, 'Jesus is Lord,' and believe in your heart that God raised Him from the dead, you will be saved. For it is with your heart that you believe and are justified, and it is with your mouth that you confess and are saved."

Which do you choose Heaven or Hell? The choice is yours. Jesus already paid the price for your sins. All you have to do is accept it.

Joshua 24:15 "But if serving the Lord seems undesirable to you, then choose for yourselves this day whom you will serve, whether the gods your forefathers served beyond the River or the gods of the Amorites, in whose land you are living. But as for me and my household, we will serve the Lord."

John 1:8-9 "If we claim to be without sin, we deceive ourselves and the truth is not in us. If we confess our sins, He is faithful and just and will forgive us our sins and purify us from all unrighteousness."

James 2:17 "In the same way, faith by itself, if it is not accompanied by action, is dead."

It is so easy to receive salvation and your name written in the Lamb's Book of Life, assuring your eternal home in heaven. You make it hard. God made it easy. He paid the price and the punishment for our sins. Just believe and receive.

What is your choice? God is faithful to all His promises.

Isaiah 46:10 "I say: My purpose will stand, and I will do all that I please."

Laziness Puts God on the Back Burner

Ecclesiastes **10:18** "If a man is lazy, the rafters sag; if his hands are idle, the house leaks."

Scripture Readings:

Exodus 29:38-43
Leviticus Chapter 1
Proverbs 6:6-11

How is your spiritual house? Do you find it lacking? Are you still in the same place spiritually that you have been in for years? Do you find that your growth in the Lord or work of the Lord has not grown or matured? Do you want to move to the next level in the Lord? What are you doing to get there? Or are you expecting God to do everything? Well, news flash, He already did it! He did it on the cross! Victory is ours in everything from salvation to our everyday trials through our Lord and Savior Jesus Christ! It is time to wake up and do your part! Do you want to move on to the next level for God? Well, do something!

Ephesians 4:14 "Wake up, O sleeper, and rise from the dead, and Christ will shine on you."

If you know what you need to be doing, you feel as if God is directing you to do something for Him, and don't do it, you make excuse after excuse, it is disobedience. This shows that God is not first in your life. If you want to move up with God, you must first put Him first! We should not hold God lightly! He is our Heavenly Father, but He is also our God! He is a God of love, but He is also our Heavenly Father who disciplines those He loves; reference (Hebrews 12:5-6).

Ephesians 5:6 "God's wrath comes on those who are disobedient."

In the Book of Exodus, the Israelites offered sacrifices in the morning and in the evening. Don't make a law about anything, but it is not difficult for us to do the same. Make your own time to have a devotion in which you pray, read the Bible, and study, but rise in the morning telling Him good morning and go to bed telling Him good night; talk to Him during the day as your heart leads you to do so. Rising with the Lord and in the evening going to bed with the Lord; how then can our day go wrong? We are to rise inviting the Lord to be with us and guide us through our day, feeding on His Word. He is our daily bread, our strength. We are to rise early to be with the Lord. He speaks to our hearts as we make time for Him before the busyness of the day starts and squeezes any time, we have left for God out and then you find you have no time for Him. God should not be the second fiddle in your life! He is the Creator of the world and Savior of your soul! Isn't He worth getting up a little earlier for? He hung on the cross for you!

Psalm 5:3 "In the morning O Lord, you hear my voice; in the morning I lay my requests before you and wait in expectation."

Judges 6:38 "Gideon rose early the next day; he squeezed the fleece and wrung out the dew - a bowlful of water."

Gideon rose *early* in the morning. Is God more important to you than your sleep? If you have no time in your busy schedule for God during the day, rise early in the morning. Make time for Him! He deserves our best! He deserves to be first and not when we can fit Him in! He died for us! He was beaten beyond human recognition for us (Isaiah 52:13-14). Can't you get up a little earlier than usual to spend some quality time with God and stop being so lazy? Or is God not important enough for you to do that? Does your sleep mean more to you than God? He is your bread and living water! Gideon rose early, and his bowl was full of water! Full of the Lord!

John 7:37-38 "If anyone is thirsty, let him come to me and drink. Whoever believes in me, as the Scripture has said, streams of living water will flow from within him."

John 6:35 "I am the Bread of Life. He who comes to me will never go hungry, and he who believes in me will never be thirsty."

Do you find yourself in a desert wasteland? Are you in a whirlwind of emotions and trials all the time and can't find any strength to get back to where you need to be or even to move forward in the Lord as you are called to do? Maybe you are not feeding on the Word of God or spending enough time with Him as you should be.

Psalm 46:1 "God is our refuge and strength, an ever-present help in times of trouble."

How much time do you devote to God? Is He important to you? Or is He your "911" God to call on when you need something?

A good relationship takes two. It is two-way not just one. It is give and take on the side of both parties involved. You cannot be selfish with God and expect Him to answer all your prayers, be a taker, and never be a giver! You will have a poor relationship with God. It will be lacking. You will be thirsty and hungry. Your spiritual house will have "leaks."
God sees all, and He knows what importance you place on Him.

Proverbs 5:21 "For a man's ways are in full view of the Lord, and He examines all his paths."

Matthew 6:21 "For where your treasure is, there your heart will be also."

Where is your treasure? Is it with God or is it on earthly things? Do you wake up wanting to tell God "Good morning!" Or is it on everything you have to do? God tells us in the Book of Leviticus chapter 23:9-14 about first fruits. He tells us because He wants to be first of all things in your life. He created us and He deserves all the respect and reverence and glory and honor and praise that we can give Him. If it were not for His grace, love, mercy, forgiveness, and sacrifice we would all be doomed to Hell!

Daniel 6:26-27 "I issue a decree that in every part of my kingdom, people must fear and reverence the God of Daniel. For He is the living God and He endures forever; His kingdom will not be destroyed, His dominion will never end. He rescues and He saves; He performs signs and wonders in the heavens and on the earth. He has rescued Daniel from the power of the lions."

Are you giving back to the Lord? Do you make time for Him? Or are you just taking? Are you a slave to the world and its desires and pleasures and troubles, or are you a slave to God? What rules you? The busyness of your day, or God?

Proverbs 12:24 "Diligent hands will rule but laziness ends in slave labor."

You do have a choice. To have an abundant life, full of God's peace, joy, and the wonderful plans He has for you, you must choose for yourself. You cannot let anyone choose for you as to who or what comes first in your life. They will not suffer the consequences. You will.

Isaiah 2:22 "Stop trusting in man, who has but a breath in his nostrils. Of what account is he?"

Acts 5:29 "We must obey God rather than men!"

God will not force Himself on you. You must choose for yourself.

Deuteronomy 30:19-20 "I have set before you life and death, blessings and curses. Now choose life, so that you and your children may live and that you may love the Lord your God, listen to His voice, and hold fast to Him. For the Lord is your life, and He will give you many years in the land He swore to give to your fathers, Abraham, Isaac, and Jacob."

The Sinful Nature Can't Inherit The Kingdom Of God

Romans 8:1-11
Galatians 5:16-21

Romans 8:5-8 "Those who live according to the sinful nature have their minds set on what that nature desires, but those who live in accordance with the Spirit have their minds set on what the Spirit desires. The mind of sinful man is death, but the mind controlled by the Spirit is life and peace; the sinful mind is hostile to God. It does not submit to God's law, nor can it do so. Those controlled by the sinful nature cannot please God."

As Paul is saying in this passage if your mind is controlled by the sinful nature, that nature within you is hostile to God. When we come to God to receive Jesus into our hearts, we must be sincere. God knows lip service. He knows our hearts.

Jeremiah 16:17 "My eyes are on all their ways; they are not hidden from me, nor is their sin concealed from my eyes."

Jeremiah 12:2-3 "You are always on their lips but far from their hearts. Yet you know me, O Lord; you see me and test my thoughts about you."

The Lord says when we receive Him, we must turn from our wicked ways. Paul is speaking here to people who think that they are Christians but, in fact, like many people sitting on our pews in the church today are a "Synagogue of Satan," (Revelation 2:9). They think that just because they asked Jesus into their hearts that they are saved, but indeed they are not! Let me remind you again of

Galatians 5:21 "Those who live like this will not inherit the Kingdom of God."

John 3:6 "No one who continues to sin has either seen Him or known Him."

John 3:9 "No one who is born of God will continue to sin, because God's seed remains in him; he cannot go on sinning, because he has been born of God."

Hebrews 6:4-6 "It is impossible for those who have once been enlightened, who have tasted the heavenly gift, who have shared in the Holy Spirit, who have tasted the goodness of the Word of God and the powers of the coming age, if they fall away, to be brought back to repentance because to their loss they are crucifying the Son of God all over again and subjecting Him to public disgrace."

Do not be deceived! Do not think yourselves so learned that you forget to continue to learn for yourself! You are still a servant of God! He is still your Father and God who will correct and discipline you if you do not heed His warnings! Lot's wife thought she was saved. She was escaping like many people today who think they are escaping by asking Jesus into their hearts but do not turn from their sinful ways. They still live in continual habitual sin rebelling against God! As in the above verse this is "hostile to God" Do not be foolish and think that you can live in this way, sinning and rebelling, which is hostile to God, and think that you can still be saved! If you never turned from your wicked ways, you would never be saved! God cannot be mocked! This kind of action is a slap in the face to everything that Jesus endured on the cross! Do you think He suffered scorn, was beaten beyond human recognition, was nailed to a cross, bore the sins of the world, and died to rise again, just so you can keep sinning? Do not be so foolish!

Galatians 6:7 "Do not be deceived: God cannot be mocked. A man reaps what he sows. The one who sows to please his sinful nature, from that nature will reap destruction; the one who sows to please the Spirit, from the Spirit will reap eternal life."

1 Corinthians 1:27 "But God chose the foolish things of the world to shame the wise."

In turning to Jesus, you must turn completely away from your life of sin. If you are still looking at your life of sin (living in and desiring the ways of the world instead of God's) how then can you be looking at Jesus? Lot's wife proved you can't. Look what happened to her. God calls us to "Be holy as I am holy," (1 Peter 1:16). He gives no exceptions. You cannot have it both ways.

Ephesians 4:22-24 "You were taught, with regard to your former way of life, to put off your old self, which is being corrupted by its deceitful desires; to be made new in the attitude of your minds; and to put on the new self, created to be like God in true righteousness and holiness."

1 Corinthians 10:21-22 "You cannot drink the cup of the Lord and the cup of demons too; you cannot have a part in both the Lord's Table and the table of demons. Are we trying to arouse the Lord's jealousy? Are we stronger than He?"

1. Sensual Sins: **Galatians 5:19** "The acts of the sinful nature are obvious: sexual immorality, impurity, and debauchery."
2. Superstitious Sins: **Galatians 5:20**

"Idolatry and witchcraft"

3. Social Sins: **Galatians 5:20-21**

"Hatred, discord, jealousy, fits of rage, selfish ambition, dissensions, factions, and envy; drunkenness, orgies, and the like. I warn you, as I did before, that those who live like this will not inherit the kingdom of God."

God knows lip service and He cannot be mocked. Going to church, singing in the choir, teaching Sunday school, etc., or even being a Pastor will not get you into heaven if your heart is not in total submission to God. He wants to be first! You cannot have Him and the ways of the world too! He is a jealous God!

Revelation 1:17 "I am the First and the Last."

Matthew 6:33 "But seek first His kingdom and His righteousness, and all these things will be given to you as well."

He says do not love the world or anything in the world.

John 2:15-17 "Do not love the world or anything in the world. If anyone loves the world, the love of the Father is not in him. For everything in the world - the cravings of sinful man, the lust of his eyes, and the boasting of what he has and does - comes not from the Father but from the world. The world and its desires pass away, but the man who does the will of God lives forever."

This leads to something else. Doing good deeds will not get you into heaven either.

Ephesians 2:8-9 "For it is by grace you have been saved, through faith - and this not from yourselves, it is the gift of God - not by works so that no one can boast. For we are God's workmanship, created in Christ Jesus to do good works, which God has prepared in   advance for us to do."

Remember as well even as Christians doing good works; consider your motive. If it is to look good in front of other people; it is to seek man's approval. Man's approval is what you will get and not God's. This is pure flesh! We are to do good works out of the love of Jesus that is within us and to please God only! We must seek God's approval and love first; in this, we will be the loving children of God to all people that God wants us to be.

Matthew 6:1-4 "Be careful not to do your 'acts of righteousness' before men, to be seen by them. If you do, you will have no reward from your Father in heaven. So, when you give to the needy, do not announce it with
Trumpets, as the hypocrites do in the synagogues and on the streets, to be honored by men. I tell you the truth; they have received their reward in full. But when you give to the needy, do not let your left hand know what your right hand is doing, so that your giving may be in secret. Then your Father, who sees what is done in secret, will reward you."

Living according to the Flesh or Sinful Nature

1. You will have unceasing conflict in your life
2. You will have repeated defeats in your life in one area or another.
3. Your growth in Christ will be stunted
4. You are unfaithful to God, and if you do not change

Galatians 5:21 "I warn you, as I did before, that those who live like this will not inherit the kingdom of God."

The only way to conquer the desires of the flesh

Galatians 5:16 "So I say, live by the Spirit, and you will not gratify the desires of the sinful nature."

John 8:11 "Go now and leave your life of sin."

Walking in the Spirit will help you to put to death the desires of the sinful nature. You will have thoughts and temptations, but when you truly are a child of God, he will give you the strength to overcome as you do his will.

First, you must:

1. Be persuaded that you can't live in your own strength. "I am the vine; you are the branches. If a man remains in me and me in him, he will bear much fruit; apart from me you can do nothing," (John 15:5).
2. Surrender to God and the Holy Spirit your whole self
3. Trust that God will do all he says that he will do

4. You must read His Word daily and put ALL of it into practice -
not just parts to suit yourself. It is your bread, your strength, and your
weapon against the sinful nature and   Satan.

Joshua 1:8 "Do not let this Book of the Law depart from your
mouth; meditate on it day and night, so that you may be careful to do
everything written in it. Then you will be prosperous and successful."

Deuteronomy 4:2 "Do not add to what I command you and do not
subtract from it but keep the commands of the Lord your God that I
give you."

Revelation 22:18 "I warn everyone who hears the words of the
prophecy of this book: If anyone adds anything to them, God will add
to him the plagues described in this book. And if anyone takes words
away from this book of prophecy, God will take away from him his share
in the tree of life and in the holy city, which is described in this book."

Indeed, the whole Bible is prophecy fulfilled.

Philippians 4:13 "I can do everything through Him who gives me
strength."

CHAPTER 3

Keep Growing: Spiritual Growth

In our physical growth, we learn and grow in maturity by experience and learning from the mistakes we make; it is the same in our spiritual growth. You may wonder from time to time why God doesn't make everything perfect and take everything bad away that Satan throws at you. Well, the answer is simple; you would not learn, and it would not be engraved into your heart the way learning from your mistakes is. "And we know that in all things God works for the good of those who love Him, who have been called according to His purpose, Romans 8:28.

The trials God allows will only be to weed out impurities, teach or correct you, and help the spiritual gifts given to you to grow and perfect. "Consider it pure joy, my brothers, whenever you face trials of many kinds because you know that the testing of your faith develops perseverance. Perseverance must finish its work so that you may be mature and complete, not lacking anything. If any of you lacks wisdom, he should ask God, who gives generously to all without finding fault, and it will be given to him," James 1:2-5. The Bible studies on the following pages will help you to learn and to understand God's purpose for allowing them.

When different situations happen in your life in which Satan wants to make you afraid, angry, and depressed, these studies will help you to learn what verses to stand on in faith and to seek out answers from God as to what He is trying to teach you. Knowing that He is a loving God and is only trying to help your faith grow and to help you become a stronger child of God will help you to face the trials and persevere through them to victory.

Get Out Of The Boat Of Doubt And Despair

To overcome you must take a step of faith

James 2:17 "In the same way, faith by itself, if it is not accompanied by action, is dead."

God gave us free will. He wants us to love and follow Him because we want to and not because we are made to. A love given out of free will is a love that is loyal and true. It is the only love worth having. That is why we must take a step toward God. When we do, He will take one toward us and help us the rest of the way. Peter was the only disciple to walk on water. He took a step of faith. The others sat in the boat and watched. I want to be in the middle of God's miracle-working power, not a watching bystander!!!

Matthew 14:25-29 "During the fourth watch of the night Jesus went out to them, walking on the lake. When the disciples saw Him walking on the lake, they were terrified. 'It's a ghost,' they said and cried out in fear. But Jesus immediately said to them: 'Take courage! It is I. Don't be afraid.' 'Lord, if it's you,' Peter replied, 'tell me to come to you on the water.' 'Come,' He said. Then Peter got down out of the boat, walked on the water, and came toward Jesus."

Are you in an overwhelming trial and cannot seem to find your way out? Take your eyes off of your problem and look to Jesus! Looking constantly at your problem doesn't fix it; it only succeeds in keeping you depressed and stealing your joy. That is the goal of Satan, and you are playing right into his hands by dwelling on your problem and staying depressed. Look to Jesus. He is the way, the only way to victory!

John 14:6 "I am the way and the truth and the life. No one comes to the Father except through Me."

Get out of the boat of doubt and despair and onto the water of faith. Just as Peter did as he got out of the boat. If you never get out of the boat, you will never walk on water. If you never look to and believe in Jesus you will not be saved. If you never trust Him and take a step of faith to believe Him for the answer to your prayers, they will not be answered. Faith without action is just lip service. Anyone can say that they believe. True faith is accompanied by action. It is your act of faith, the action you take that backs up your faith and what you believe for that releases the power of God.

James 2:22 "You see that his faith and his actions were working together, and his faith was made complete by what he did."

Philippians 4:13 "I can do everything through Him who gives me strength."

If would only believe, God will give you the strength to do what you must do. If you are looking for a job, go out looking with a positive attitude believing that you will get one. If believing for a pay raise, tithe in advance for the amount of the pay raise you are expecting. If believing for a lost loved one to be saved, treat them with love while waiting for God to direct their steps. Keep praying. Whether they read it or not, they will when they finally answer God's call. Do not preach at them. Give them over to God. Let God be God!! He convicts. Not us. Jesus came to save the world, not to condemn. So who are we to do it? God says, in everything, to do it in love. Love overcomes all evil. God loved us first. We must love others first just as He does. Love carries no bitterness or resentment. True love will penetrate their heart. His love and patience brought us to Him. Our love and patience along with God's will; will bring our lost loved ones to Christ.

John: 6 "As you have heard from the beginning, His command is that you walk in love."

John 4:7-11 "Dear friends, let us love one another, for love comes from God. Everyone who loves has been born of God and knows God. Whoever does not love does not know God, because God is love. This is how God showed His love among us: He sent His One and Only Son into the world so that we might live through Him. This is love: not that we loved God, but that He loved us and sent His Son as an atoning sacrifice for our sins. Dear friends, since God so loved us, we also ought to love one another."

Romans 12:21 "Do not be overcome by evil but overcome evil with good."

1 Corinthians 13:4-8 "Love is patient, love is kind. It does not envy, it does not boast, it is not proud. It is not rude, it is not self-seeking, it is not easily angered, and it keeps no record of wrongs. Love does not delight in evil but rejoices with the truth. It always protects, always trusts, always hopes, always perseveres. Love never fails"

God is faithful. His timing is not ours - wait in faith!

God is faithful and will answer our prayers but in His time. Not ours. He is not a vending machine that we can go put in our requests and He will pop out the answers. Trust Him and show Him the same patience that He shows you. Keep waiting in faith.

Psalm 145:13 "The Lord is faithful to all His promises and loving toward all He has made."

Psalm 27:14 "Wait for the Lord; be strong and take heart and wait for the Lord."

Ecclesiastes 8:6 "For there is a proper time and procedure for every matter, though a man's misery weighs heavily upon him."

The moment Peter took his eyes off Jesus he started to sink and became afraid. That is because he was not looking to Jesus and the strength that He gives. Jesus is the author and perfecter of our faith. Even though Peter started to sink, Jesus still helped him up. He will do the same for you.

Matthew 14:30-31 "But when he saw the wind, he was afraid and, beginning to sink, cried out, 'Lord save me!' Immediately Jesus reached out His hand and caught him. 'You have little faith,' He said, 'why did you doubt?'"

Hebrews 12:2-3 "Let us fix our eyes on Jesus, the author, and perfecter of our faith, who for the joy set before Him endured the cross, scorning its shame, and sat down at the right hand of the throne of God. Consider Him who endured such opposition from sinful men, so that you will not grow weary and lose heart."

There is no fear in Jesus. Fear is not from God but from the enemy. Victory, courage, and strength are found in Jesus!

Romans 8:15 "For you did not receive a spirit that makes you a slave again to fear, but you received the Spirit of sonship. And by Him we cry, '*Abba*,' Father."

Psalm 73:26 "My flesh and my heart may fail, but God is the strength of my heart and my portion forever."

Psalm 138:3 "When I called, you answered me; you made me bold and stouthearted."

Victory is ours as we trust in and obey the words of Jesus Christ.

1 Corinthians 15:57-58 "He gives us the victory through our Lord Jesus Christ. Therefore, my dear brothers, stand firm. Always give yourselves fully to the work of the Lord, because you know that your labor in the Lord is not in vain."

There will be times due to attacks from Satan that you stumble as Peter did. But take heart, Jesus overcame the world and will be there to pick you up as He did for Peter.

John 16:33 "I have told you these things, so that in me you may have peace. In this world, you will have trouble. But take heart! I have overcome the world."

Psalm 91:14 "Because he loves me,' says the Lord, 'I will rescue him; I will protect him, for he acknowledges my name."

Deuteronomy 31:6 "He will never leave you nor forsake you."

Psalm 145:14 "The Lord upholds all those who fall and lifts up all who are bowed down."

God will always be there to catch you when you fall. But you have to get out of the boat. At least Peter got out. Dead faith will not release God's power. The other disciples stayed in and did not experience God's awesome power that helped Peter to walk on water. Peter did.

James 2:26 "As the body without the spirit is dead, so faith without deeds is dead."

Our faith is not judged in our momentary weaknesses, in our falling down. It is in perseverance, the getting back up, and continuing on. It takes great faith to get back up and keep going, to keep believing even when you stumble.

Hebrews 12:1 "Therefore, since we are surrounded by such a great cloud of witnesses, let us throw off everything that hinders and the sin that so easily entangles, and let us run with perseverance the race marked out for us."

Philippians 3:13-14 "Brothers, I do not consider myself yet to have taken hold of it. But one thing I do: Forgetting what is behind and straining toward what is ahead, I press on toward the goal to win the prize for which God has called me heavenward in Christ Jesus."

James 1:12 "Blessed is the man who perseveres under trial, because when he has stood the test, he will receive the crown of life that God has promised to those who love Him."

James 5:10-11 "Brothers, as an example of patience in the face of suffering, take the prophets who spoke in the name of the Lord. As you know, we consider blessed those who have persevered. You have heard of Job's perseverance and have seen what the Lord finally brought about. The Lord is full of compassion and mercy."

Everyone can have faith when everything is going well. True faith stands the test during the trials and hard times when everything looks or appears to be bad, dead, or over.

1 Peter 1:6-7 "In this you greatly rejoice, though now for a little while you may have had to suffer grief in all kinds of trials. These have come so that your faith - of greater worth than gold, which perishes even though refined by fire - may be proved genuine and may result in praise, glory, and honor when Jesus Christ is revealed."

Jesus had to die before He could be raised from the dead. Lazarus died, and Jesus brought him back to life. We have to die to ourselves to our old life of habitual sin to receive salvation and eternal life. What do you have that looks dead, a job, a marriage, your finances, or a dream? Don't give up when Jesus can resurrect it. If He could be raised from the dead, He can certainly raise whatever is dead in your life. Have faith and you will rise! Whatever is dead in your life will rise again if you keep believing; don't give up! You will see victory, but only if you persevere. Stand firm until the victory is complete. Jesus will keep you strong. God is glorified in healing the sick, but He is glorified even more in raising the dead!!!

Hebrews 11:6 "And without faith it is impossible to please God."

Isaiah 7:9 "If you do not stand firm in your faith, you will not stand at all."

1 Corinthians 1:8-9 "He will keep you strong to the end so that you will be blameless on the day of our Lord Jesus Christ. God, who has called you into fellowship with his Son Jesus Christ our Lord, is faithful."

Jesus is faithful and will fulfill every promise.

Philippians 1:6 "Being confident of this, that He who began a good work in you will carry it on to completion until the day of Christ Jesus."

Psalm 119:105 "Your Word is a lamp to my feet and a light for my path."

Hold on to God's Word. Read it and let His Word speak to your heart and stand on His promises. God calls things that are not as though they already exist. He speaks them first, then they manifest.

John 6:47-48 "I tell you the truth; he who believes has everlasting life. I am the bread of life."

Psalm 138:2 "For you have exalted above all things your Name and Your Word."

Romans 4:17-18 "The God who gives life to the dead and calls things that are not as though they were. Against all hope, Abraham in hope believed and so became the father of many nations."

Jesus was prophesied throughout the Old Testament. Noah built the Ark, and then the rain came. Humble yourself and seek God's will and strength. He will gladly give you the answer to your prayers. He wants to bless you. Know that God is in control.

Jeremiah 29:11 "For I know the plans I have for you,' declares the Lord, 'plans to prosper you and not to harm you, plans to give you hope and a future.'"

Proverbs 20:24 "A man's steps are directed by the Lord. How then can anyone understand his own way."

John 14:12-14 "I tell you the truth, anyone who has faith in Me will do what I have been doing. He will do even greater things than these because I am going to the Father. And I will do whatever you ask in My name, so that the Son may bring glory to the Father. You may ask Me for anything in My name, and I will do it."

1 Peter 5:6-11 "Humble yourselves, therefore, under God's might hand, that He may lift you up in due time. Cast all your anxiety on Him because He cares for you. Be self-controlled and alert. Your enemy the devil prowls around like a roaring lion looking for someone to devour. Resist him, standing firm in the faith, because you know that your brothers throughout the world are undergoing the same kind of suffering. And the God of all grace, who called you to His eternal glory in Christ, after you have suffered a little while, will Himself restore you and make you strong, firm, and steadfast. To Him be the power forever and ever. Amen."

Believe God and let Him be God and do His job. He does not need us to tell Him or help Him. He is God. Just trust and obey. Your greatest weakness will stop your greatest desire if you let it. Recognize the areas that you are weak in and ask God for the strength to endure and overcome. Focus on God and His awesome power and love. Focus on the things that He has already brought you through.

James 4:2 "You do not have, because you do not ask God."

Philippians 4:6-9 "Do not be anxious about anything, but in everything, by prayer and petition with thanksgiving, present your requests to God. And the peace of God, which transcends all understanding, will guard your hearts and your minds in Christ Jesus. Finally, brothers, whatever is true, whatever is noble, whatever is right, whatever is pure, whatever is lovely, whatever is admirable - if anything is excellent or praiseworthy - think about such things. Whatever you have learned or received or heard from me, or seen in me - put it into practice. And the God of peace will be with you."

Ephesians 6:13 "Therefore put on the full armor of God, so that when the day of evil comes, you may be able to stand your ground, and after you have done everything, to stand."

Psalm 46:10-11 "Be still and know that I am God. I will be exalted among the nations; I will be exalted in earth. The Lord Almighty is with us; the God of Jacob is our fortress."

You're praying, you're obeying God's Word; you're reading and studying the Word - Yet still waiting. Then wait in faith. Waiting and complaining is not waiting in faith.

Psalm 31:24 "Be strong and take heart, all you who hope in the Lord."

Your prayer will be answered if you wait in faith. Stand on the Word. Pray it and believe it.

Mark 11:24 "Therefore I tell you, whatever you ask for in prayer, believe that you have received it, and it will be yours."

Ephesians 6:10-11 "Finally, be strong in the Lord and in His mighty power. Put on the full armor of God so that you can take your stand against the devil's schemes."

God is a God of miracles. Trust in God. He is a God of love.

Psalm 77:13-14 "Your ways, O God, are holy. What god is so great as our God? You are the God who performs miracles; You display Your power among the peoples."

John 4:16 "And so we know and rely on the love God has for us. God is love. Whoever lives in love lives in God, and God in him."

Let His perfect love guard your heart and drive your fears away. Trust in God to keep you strong and able to endure through all of your trials to ensure victory. Look to God in everything.

John 4:18 "There is no fear in love. But perfect love drives out fear because fear has to do with punishment. The one who fears is not made perfect in love."

Psalm 34:4 "I sought the Lord, and He answered me; He delivered me from all my fears."

He may not answer in the way and time you expect, but He will answer and deliver you better than you can imagine.

Ecclesiastes 3:1 "There is a time for everything and a season for every activity under heaven."

God will answer your prayers because he loves you and for his glory. When His glory touches your life and those around you. The glory of God causes all who are touched to die to self and live in Christ. The glory of God brings forth God's power and answers your prayers. When the glory of God came down and shook open the prison doors in Acts 16, everyone's chains came loose, and the jailer was saved because of it.

Acts 16:26 "Suddenly there was such a violent earthquake that the foundations of the prison were shaken. At once all the prison doors flew open, and everybody's chains came loose."

Acts 16:34 "The jailer brought them into his house and set a meal before them; he was filled with joy because he had come to believe in God - he and his whole family."

Isaiah 42:7 "To open eyes that are blind, to free captives from prison and to release from the dungeon those who sit in darkness."

Isaiah 48:11 "For My own sake, for My own sake, I do this. How can I let Myself be defamed? I will not yield My glory to another."

Isaiah 55:8-9 "For My thoughts are not your thoughts, neither are your ways My ways,' declares the Lord. 'As the heavens are higher than the earth, so are My ways higher than your ways and My thoughts than your thoughts."

Isaiah 55:11-12 "So is My Word that goes out from my mouth: It will not return to me empty but will accomplish what I desire and achieve the purpose for which I sent it. You will go out in joy and be led forth in peace."

Psalm 102:15 "The nations will fear the name of the Lord, all the kings of the earth will revere your glory."

1 Corinthians 10:31 "So whether you eat or drink or whatever you do, do it all for the glory of God."

Deuteronomy 5:24-25 "The Lord our God has shown us His glory and His majesty, and we have heard His voice from the fire. Today we have seen that a man can live even if God speaks with him. But now, why should we die? This great fire will consume us, and we will die if we hear the voice of the Lord our God any longer."

Hold on to God and His Word. It is your strength to overcome, your ammunition against Satan.

Isaiah 30:15 "In repentance and rest is your salvation; in quietness and trust is your strength."

Psalm 29:11 "The Lord gives strength to His people; the Lord blesses His people with peace."

Psalm 149:6-7 "May the praise of God be in their mouths and a double-edged sword in their hands, to inflict vengeance on the nations and punishment on the peoples, to bind their kings with fetters, their nobles with shackles of iron, to carry out the sentence written against them. This is the glory of all His saints."

Ephesians 6:12 "For our struggle is not against flesh and blood, but against the rulers, against the authorities, against the powers of this dark world and against the spiritual forces of evil in the heavenly realms."

Ephesians 6:14-17 "Stand firm then, with the belt of truth buckled around your waist, with the breastplate of righteousness in place, and with your feet fitted with the readiness that comes from the gospel of peace. In addition to all this, take up the shield of faith, with which you can extinguish all the flaming arrows of the evil one. Take the helmet of salvation and the sword of the Spirit, which is the Word of God."

Standing firm and praising God will bring you victory!

John 5:4-5 "For everyone born of God overcomes the world. This is the victory that overcomes the world, even our faith. Who is it that overcomes the world? Only he who believes that Jesus is the Son of God."

Psalm 50:14-15 "Sacrifice thank offerings to God, fulfill your vows to the Most High, and call upon me in the day of trouble; I will deliver you and you will honor me."

Even when your dream, finances, marriage, or job looks dead, keep believing. Remember Lazarus, and as Jesus raised him from the dead, He will raise whatever is dead in your life. You will see victory! Look at every trial as an opportunity to see the majesty, power, and glory of God displayed in your life.

2 Thessalonians 1:11-12 "We constantly pray for you, that our God may count you worthy of His calling, and that by His power He may fulfill every good purpose of yours and every act prompted by your faith. We pray this so that the name of our Lord Jesus may be glorified in you, and you in Him, according to the grace of our God and the Lord Jesus Christ."

Romans 8:17-18 "Now if we are children, then we are heirs - heirs of God and co-heirs with Christ, if indeed we share in His sufferings in order that we may also share in His glory. I consider that our present sufferings are not worth comparing with the glory that will be revealed in us."

The one and only Jesus Christ, who is in us is greater than the one who is in the world, Satan. **In Jesus Christ, we always win!**

John 4:4 "The One who is in you is greater than the one who is in the world."

Get out of the boat of despair. Have faith in God and you will be victorious!

Psalm 60:12 "With God we will gain the victory, and He will trample down our enemies."

Psalm 44:6-8 "I do not trust in my bow, my sword does not bring me victory; but you give us victory over our enemies, you put our adversaries to shame. In God, we make our boast all day long, and we will praise your name forever."

Deuteronomy 20:4 "For the Lord your God is the One who goes with you to fight for you against your enemies to give you victory."

Job 12:13-16 "To God belong wisdom and power; counsel and understanding are His. What He tears down cannot be rebuilt; the man He imprisons cannot be released. If He holds back the waters, there is drought; if He lets them loose, they devastate the land. To Him belong strength and victory; both deceived and deceiver are His."

The Righteous Will Live By Faith

R omans 1:17

Through your Christian walk on earth, you will experience hardship and trials. Jesus experienced them, and we are not above Him so we should be omitted from them. "In this, you greatly rejoice, though now for a little while you may have had to suffer grief in all kinds of trials. These have come so that your faith - of greater worth than gold, which perishes even though refined by fire - may be proven genuine and may result in praise, glory, and honor when Jesus Christ is revealed," (1 Peter 1:6-7). Your trials also strengthen you, enabling you to persevere. "Consider it pure joy, my brothers, whenever you face trials of many kinds because you know that the testing of your faith develops perseverance. Perseverance must finish its work so that you may be mature and complete, not lacking anything" James 1:2-4. Jesus is the *lion of the tribe of Judah* and not a mouse. We are to be lions as well. "Then one of the elders said to me, 'Do not weep! See, the Lion of the tribe of Judah, the Root of David, has triumphed," (Revelation 5:5).

As you walk through your trials, overcoming them in victory, your faith, love, and devotion for Jesus Christ deepens. You walk through them in faith, knowing that God will lead you through to victory.

Psalm 23:4 "Even though I walk through the valley of the shadow of death, I will fear no evil, for you are with me; your rod and your staff, they comfort me."

Psalm 60:12 "With God we will gain the victory, and He will trample down our enemies."

2 Corinthians 5:7 "We live by faith, not by sight."

Noah and the Ark

Hebrews 11:7 "By faith Noah, when warned about things not yet seen, in holy fear built an ark to save his family. By his faith, he condemned the world and became heir of the righteousness that comes by faith."

Romans 4:17 "The God who gives life to the dead and calls things that are not as though they were."

This is true faith. Faith believes even when things look their worst. Faith makes what you are hoping and believing for a reality.

Hebrews 11:1 "Now faith is the substance of things hoped for, the evidence of things not seen."

Just as Abraham believed when he was 100 yrs. Old that he would have children because God said so. He believed in God's Word, and we must believe also if we want victory in every trial.

Romans 4:18 "Against all hope, Abraham in hope believed and so became the father of many nations, just as it had been said to him."

Hebrews 11:1 "Now faith is being sure of what we hope for and certain of what we do not see."

Faith makes what you hope and pray for a reality. Faith pleases God.

Hebrews 11:6 "And without faith it is impossible to please God, because anyone who comes to Him must believe that He exists and that He rewards those who earnestly seek Him."

As your faith grows, so does your devotion and obedience to God, which also brings you victory and the blessings of the Lord.

Matthew 15:28 "Woman, you have great faith! Your request is granted."

Isaiah 1:19 "If you are willing and obedient, you will eat the best from the land; but if you resist and rebel, you will be devoured by the sword. For the mouth of the Lord has spoken."

Romans 1:5 "Through Him and for His name's sake, we received grace and apostleship to call people from among all the Gentiles to the obedience that comes from faith."

The most important part of increasing your faith is reading the Word every day. Before we receive Jesus as Lord and Savior, we have many years of the "world" in our minds. Our hearts are made new, but our minds need to be renewed. This is a daily process of reading the Word of God.

Ezekiel 36:26 "I will give you a new heart and put a new spirit in you; I will remove from you your heart of stone and give you a heart of flesh."

Romans 12:2 "Do not conform any longer to the pattern of this world but be transformed by the renewing of your mind."

Joshua 1:8 "Do not let the Book of the Law depart from your mouth; meditate on it day and night, so that you may be careful to do everything written in it. Then you will be prosperous and successful."

We are to meditate on the Word and study it. Study it by the topical concordance such as trust, faith, and faithfulness, especially topics dealing with the trials that you are going through, or just study each Book as you read through the Bible. As you study the Word and read it, God will speak to you through it. A Scripture will just light up and almost jump off the page and a feeling of warmth will go through your heart. You will know that God is speaking directly to you. Highlight those Scriptures and write them down. God will bring these Scriptures to your remembrance as you need them and they will lift your spirits. As we keep close to God in prayer and through His Word, He will keep us in peace. This will help us to trust Him more.

John 14:26 "But the Counselor, the Holy Spirit, whom the Father will send in My name, will teach you all things and will remind you of everything I have said to you."

Psalm 1:1-3 "Blessed is the man who does not walk in the counsel of the wicked or stand in the way of sinners or sit in the seat of mockers. But his delight is in the law of the Lord, and on His law he meditates day and night. He is like a tree planted by streams of water, which yields its fruit in season and whose leaf does not wither. Whatever he does prospers."

Isaiah 26:3 "You will keep in perfect peace him whose mind is steadfast, because he trusts in You."

Faith plus the Word of God: living and believing it equals peace and joy of God; rest.

Hebrews 4:2-3 "but the message they heard was of no value to them, because those who heard did not combine it with faith. Now we who have believed enter that rest, just as God has said, 'So I declared on oath in My anger, 'They shall never enter My rest.'"

Psalm 29:11 "The Lord gives strength to His people; the Lord blesses His people with peace."

Psalm 119:165 "Great peace have they who love your law, and nothing can make them stumble."

Jeremiah 6:16 "Stand at the crossroads and look; ask for the ancient paths, ask where the good way is, and walk in it, and you will find rest for your souls."

As you read the Word of God and start to learn the will and promises of God for your life it will help you to resist the devil and the thoughts he tries to attack you with to bring you down. The only way to truly resist the devil is to trust and obey God, and to read His Word daily. As you read His Word, your faith grows as you learn about the love and promises He has for you. Knowing His promises and trusting in them will give you the power to fight off Satan's attacks.

James 1:17 "Every good and perfect gift is from above."

2 Corinthians 10:5 "We demolish arguments and every pretension that sets itself up against the knowledge of God, and we take captive every thought to make it obedient to Christ."

James 4:7-8 "Submit yourselves, then, to God. Resist the devil, and he will flee from you. Come near to God and He will come near to you."

Psalm 37:4 "Delight yourself in the Lord and He will give you the desires of your heart."

Romans 10:17 "Faith comes from hearing the message, and the message is heard through the Word of Christ."

As your faith in God grows, you grow stronger as a Christian and are more able to stand against the "fiery darts" of Satan. Jesus Christ is the Rock, the foundation on which our faith is built.

Luke 6:47-48 "I will show you what he is like who comes to me and hears My Words and puts them into practice. He is like a man building a house, who dug down deep and laid the foundation on rock. When a flood came, the torrent struck that house but could not shake it, because it was well built."

Isaiah 28:16 "See, I lay a stone in Zion, a tested stone, a precious cornerstone for a sure foundation; the one who trusts will never be dismayed."

Part of putting God's Word into practice is living it, but it is also speaking it. Speak words of faith to your mountain (debt, lost loved one, etc.) and not doubt. Take the authority and dominion that God has already given you. If you speak doubt and discouragement that is what you will believe and what you will have. God's Word is living and active. As you pray the Word and speak it, believe it. The Lord says that He will never forsake us and those who trust in Him will never be put to shame. So believe in remembering what God says He will do, He will do. Also, remember that He never promises immediate answers. Some of our prayers take time. Keep trusting and keep praying.

Genesis 1:26 "Let us make man in our image, in our likeness, and let them rule over the fish of the sea and the birds of the air, over the livestock, over all the earth, and over all the creatures that move along the ground."

Matthew 10:1 "He called His twelve disciples to Him and gave them authority to drive out evil spirits and to heal every disease and sickness." *Every disease or sickness includes physical, spiritual, or emotional.*

Matthew 21:21-22 "I tell you the truth, if you have faith and do not doubt, not only can you do what was done to the fig tree, but also you can say to this mountain, 'Go, throw yourself into the sea,' and it will be done. If you believe, you will receive whatever you ask for in prayer."

Mark 11:24 "Therefore I tell you, whatever you ask for in prayer, believe that you have received it, and it will be yours."

Romans 10:11 "Anyone who trusts in Him will **never** be put to shame."

Hebrews 4:12 "For the Word of God is living and active. Sharper than any double-edged sword, it penetrates even to dividing soul and spirit, joints and marrow; it judges the thoughts and attitudes of the heart."

Isaiah 55:11 "So is My Word that goes out from my mouth: It will not return to me empty but will accomplish what I desire and achieve the purpose for which I sent it."

2 Samuel 22:31 " As for God, His way is perfect; the Word of the Lord is flawless."

Ecclesiastes 8:6 "For there is a proper time and procedure for every matter, though a man's misery weighs heavily upon him."

There is a proper time for everything and only one successful way, God's way. God's way is seed time and harvest. Whatever you sow is what you will reap. Whatever you need or want, give and it will be given unto you; whether it is love, understanding, mercy, forgiveness, money, or friendship. Remember just as a farmer plants and it takes time for his harvest to start growing, so it is when you sow unto the Lord.

Mark 4:26-29 "This is what the kingdom of God is like. A man scatters seed on the ground. Night and day, whether he sleeps or gets up, the seed sprouts and grows, though he does not know how. All by itself the soil produces grain - first the stalk, then the head, then the full kernel in the head. As soon as the grain is ripe, he puts the sickle to it, because the harvest has come.”

1 Corinthians 3:7 “So neither he who plants nor he who waters is anything, but only God, who makes things grow.”

Galatians 6:7-8 “A man reaps what he sows. The one who sows to please his sinful nature, from that nature will reap destruction; the one who sows to please the Spirit, from the Spirit will reap eternal life.”

Luke 6:38 “Give and it will be given to you. A good measure, pressed down, shaken together, and running over, will be poured into your lap. For with the measure you use, it will be measured to you.”

Trust in God as His word tells us:

Proverbs 3:5-6 “Trust in the Lord with all your heart and lean not on your own understanding; in all your ways acknowledge Him, and He will make your paths straight.”

Part of acknowledging God is making Him Lord of your whole self and life, and worshiping Him for who He is, God! He is the Creator of heaven and earth and everything in it. Part of true worship is to love, trust, and obey Him. All of this acknowledges God for who He is. As you do this you will live in and walk in the fruit of His Spirit. This is God’s way of doing things. Seek God first and His Kingdom, or His way of doing things and He will take care of everything else that you need.

Matthew 6:33 “But seek first His kingdom and His righteousness, and all these things will be given to you as well.”

Galatians 5:16 "So I say, live by the Spirit, and you will not gratify the desires of the sinful nature."

Philippians 4:19 "And my God will meet all your needs according to His glorious riches in Christ Jesus."

1 Peter 1:16 "Be holy, because I am holy."

Deuteronomy 11:22-23 "If you carefully observe all these commands, I am giving you to follow - to love the Lord your God, to walk in all His ways and to hold fast to Him - then the Lord will drive out all these nations before you, and you will dispossess nations larger and stronger than you."

The diligence that you show in continually reading and living out the Word of God and walking in faith by the Spirit of God, you will make your hope sure and strengthen your faith even more.

Hebrews 6:11-12 "We want each of you to show this same diligence to the very end, in order to make your hope sure. We do not want you to become lazy, but to imitate those who through faith and patience inherit what has been promised."

Your faith, patience, and willingness to wait on God.

Psalm 46:10 "Be still, and know that I am God," to let God be God and work out the answer to your prayers will cause you to inherit what God has promised you.

Psalm 145:13 "God is faithful to all His promises and loving toward all He has made."

Hebrews 6:17-19 "Because God wanted to make the unchanging nature of His purpose very clear to the heirs of what was promised, He confirmed it with an oath. God did this so that, by two unchangeable things in which it is impossible for God to lie, we who have fled to take hold of the hope offered to us may be greatly encouraged. We have this hope as an anchor for the soul, firm and secure."

God gave us His Word as a source of strength and encouragement, and to help guide our path in life. He did this out of His undying love for us. His Word is just one of the ways in which God has shown His love for us and provided for us.

Joshua 1:5 "I will never leave you nor forsake you."

Psalm 32:8 "I will instruct you and teach you in the way you should go; I will counsel you and watch over you."

Numbers 23:19 "God is not a man, that He should lie, nor a son of man, that He should change His mind. Does He speak and then not act? Does He promise and not fulfill?"

Joshua 21:43-45 "So the Lord gave Israel all the land He had sworn to give their forefathers, and they took possession of it and settled there. The Lord gave them rest on every side, just as He had sworn to their forefathers. Not one of their enemies withstood them; the Lord handed all their enemies over to them. Not one of all the Lord's good promises to the house of Israel failed; every one was fulfilled."

Psalm 36:5 "Your love O Lord, reaches to the heavens, your faithfulness to the skies."

Revelation 22:11-12 "Let him who is holy continue to be holy. Behold, I am coming soon! My reward is with me, and I will give to every one according to what he has done.

God's Majestic Voice: Do You Hear It?

Have you ever prayed to hear the voice of God? How can you hear what by your own actions you have put at a distance? Have you thought of what you are really praying for when you pray to God to hear His voice more clearly? To hear Him more clearly the things in the way have to move!

James 4:7-8 "Submit yourselves, then, to God. Resist the devil, and he will flee from you. Come near to God and He will come near to you."

How can you hear someone if they are miles away? If you want to hear God more clearly then you need to turn the volume of the world and its desires off!

John 2:15-17 "Do not love the world or anything in the world. If anyone loves the world, the love of the Father is not in him. For everything in the world - the cravings of sinful man, the lust of his eyes, and the boasting of what he has and does - comes not from the Father but from the world. The world and its desires pass away, but the man who does the will of God lives forever."

The volume of the "what about me's," and the "I wants" and the cravings your flesh controls whether in action, speech, or food off! It is in between you and God! Don't keep Him at a distance! You will hear Him more clearly.

Galatians 5:16-21 "So I say, live by the Spirit, and you will not gratify the desires of the sinful nature. For the sinful nature desires what is contrary to the Spirit, and the Spirit what is contrary to the sinful nature. But if you are led by the Spirit, you are not under the law. The acts of the sinful nature are obvious: sexual immorality, impurity, and debauchery; idolatry and witchcraft; hatred, discord, jealousy, fits of rage, selfish ambition, dissensions, factions, and envy; drunkenness, orgies, and the like. I warn you, as I did before, that those who live like this will not inherit the kingdom of God."

How can you hear God when your focus is not on Him? How can you hear Him when directly in front of your thoughts and desires you have placed your own self-centered desires that have no eternal value at all? Someone once said to only "fight fights worth fighting." Is what you focus on daily something that will make a difference in heaven, give you a testimony, or win someone to Christ? When your focus is on yourself and your own needs and what the world desires or expects how can it be on God?

Galatians 1:10 "Am I now trying to win the approval of men, or of God?"

If you keep God the main and only focus of your life He will take care of the rest. It is okay to want other things, just don't let them control you.

Matthew 6:33 "But seek first the His kingdom and His righteousness, and all these things will be given to you as well."

Hebrews 12:1-3 "Therefore, since we are surrounded by such a great cloud of witnesses, let us throw off everything that hinders and the sin that so easily entangles, and let us run with perseverance the race marked out for us. Let us fix our eyes on Jesus, the author and perfecter of our faith, who for the joy set before him endured the cross, scorning its shame, and sat down at the right hand of the throne of God. Consider him who endured such opposition from sinful men, so that you will not grow weary and lose heart. In your struggle against sin, you have not yet resisted to the point of shedding your blood."

Don't be afraid to trust God. Let go and let God. "He will never leave you nor forsake you.

Deuteronomy 31:8 "The Lord Himself goes before you and will be with you; He will never leave you nor forsake you. Do not be afraid; do not be discouraged."

Don't just get a revelation of this and say you are going to stay focused on God. You must put it into action!

Isaiah 29:13 "These people come near to Me with their mouth and honor Me with their lips, but their hearts are far from Me."

God does know lip service. Lip service is nothing if your actions do not back it up.

James 2:17 "In the same way, faith by itself, if it is not accompanied by action, is dead."

The wisdom of God displayed in you and your sincerity to obey Him is proven in your actions.

Matthew 11:19 "But wisdom is proved right by her actions."

Do not just read the Word, hear a good word and a revelation preached to you and say, "Wow, I get it and I needed to hear that!" Do it! The reward of God's presence, hearing His voice, and knowing that you have a one-on-one relationship with Him is in you putting what you have heard or read into action. When you take the distance away from you and God by your own self-centered desires and to be like the world, then you will hear His voice within your heart as if you were truly face to face with Him.

Jeremiah 17:10 "I the Lord search the heart and examine the mind, to reward a man according to his conduct, according to what his deeds deserve."

Need A Word? You Reap What You Sow!

Galatians 6:7-9 "A man reaps what he sows. The one who sows to please his sinful nature, from that nature will reap destruction; the one who sows to please the Spirit, from the Spirit will reap eternal life. Let us not become weary in doing well, for at the proper time we will reap a harvest if we do not give up."

Are you going through a trying time? Do you need a Word from God? Are you in need of encouragement? Take your eyes off of the situation and yourself and put them back on Jesus. If you need encouragement, do something for someone else, encourage someone else, give and it will be given unto you. If you need a Word from God, how much time are you giving to Him? If you do not give Him any of your day, how then, can you hear from Him?

Psalm 149:6 "May the praise of God be in their mouths and a double-edged sword in their hands."

Ezra 7:9-10 "For the gracious hand of his God was on him. For Ezra had devoted himself to the study and observance of the Law of the Lord, and to teaching its decrees and laws in Israel."

2 Timothy 2:15 "Study to shew thyself approved unto God, a workman that needs not to be ashamed, rightly dividing the Word of truth."

Draw near to God in sincere love.

Your relationship with God should not be a "911" relationship. It should not be one in which the only time you come to God is to ask Him for something. He does want you to ask for whatever you need, but He also wants your love and devotion; your gratitude and glory, and praise and honor for who He is! The Almighty Creator and Savior!

Hebrews 10:22 "Let us draw near to God with a sincere heart in full assurance of faith, having our hearts sprinkled to cleanse us from a guilty conscience and having our bodies washed with pure water."

Psalm 37:4 "Delight yourself in the Lord and He will give you the desires of your heart."

Everyone needs encouragement. God knows that and wants to bless and encourage you. He wants to give you hope, but even God does not want to be taken for granted! As you draw near to God in love and faith, trusting in His love for you, you will find the strength to continue. You will see as time passes that God will supply your needs. Keep your eyes on Jesus and not on the situation. Start doing for others and you will see what you give to others will come back to you.

Psalm 27:13-14 "I am still confident of this: I will see the goodness of the Lord in the land of the living. Wait for the Lord; be strong and take heart and wait for the Lord."

Luke 6:31-32 "Do to others as you would have them do to you. If you love those who love you, what credit is that to you? Even 'sinners' love those who love them."

Luke 6:38 "Give and it will be given to you. A good measure, pressed down, shaken together, and running over, will be poured into your lap. For with the measure you use, it will be measured to you."

Jeremiah 29:11-14 " For I know the plans I have for you, declares the Lord, plans to prosper you and not to harm you, plans to give you hope and a future. Then you will call upon Me and come and pray to Me, and I will listen to you. You will seek Me and find Me when you seek Me with all your heart. I will be found by you, declares the Lord, and bring you back from captivity."

Philippians 4:13 "I can do everything through Him who gives me strength."

Philippians 4:19 "And my God will meet all your needs according to His glorious riches in Christ Jesus."

If God created us in His image, then the emotions and needs we have come from Him. He wants our love as we want His. God understands that we need to be encouraged from time to time due to the trials of life. Stay close to Him, praying and reading the Word. Do not neglect going to church. We need the fellowship of other believers. They are also a great encouragement.

Hebrews 10:25 "Let us not give up meeting together, as some are in the habit of doing, but let us encourage one another - and all the more as you see the Day approaching."

Psalm 147:5 "Great is our Lord and mighty in power; His understanding has no limit."

Palm 10:17-18 "You hear, O Lord, the desire of the afflicted; you encourage them, and you listen to their cry, defending the fatherless and the oppressed, in order that man, who is of the earth, may terrify no more."

Psalm 62:5-8 "Find rest, O my soul, in God alone; my hope comes from Him. He alone is my Rock and my Salvation; He is my fortress; I will not be shaken. My salvation and my honor depend on God; He is my mighty Rock, my refuge. Trust in Him at all times, O people; pour out your hearts to Him, for God is our refuge."

Matthew 11:28-30 "Come to me, all you who are weary and burdened, and I will give you rest. Take my yoke upon you and learn from me, for I am gentle and humble in heart, and you will find rest for your souls. For My yoke is easy and my burden is light."

2 Corinthians 1:3-4 "Praise be to the God and Father of our Lord Jesus Christ, the Father of compassion and the God of all comfort, who comforts us in all our troubles so that we can comfort those in any trouble with the comfort we ourselves have received from God."

God is our everlasting peace. As you choose to trust Him, He will give you peace and victory. The world will not. The things of this world are temporary and will perish. God will not, nor will He ever forsake you because He is love and love never fails or lets you down.

Deuteronomy 31:6 "Be strong and courageous. Do not be afraid or terrified because of them, for the Lord your God goes with you; He will never leave you nor forsake you."

John 4:16 "God is love."

1 Corinthians 13:8 "Love never fails."

John 2:15-17 "Do not love the world or anything in the world. If anyone loves the world, the love of the Father is not in him. For everything in the world - the cravings of sinful man, the lust of his eyes, and the boasting of what he has and does - comes not from the Father but from the world. The world and its desires pass away, but the man who does the will of God lives forever."

Psalm 60:12 "With God we will gain the victory, and he will trample down our enemies."

Psalm 147:12-14 "Extol the Lord, O Jerusalem; praise your God, O Zion, for He strengthens the bars of your gates and blesses your people within you. He grants peace to your borders and satisfies you with the finest of wheat."

Psalm 91:1-4 "He who dwells in the shelter of the Most High will rest in the shadow of the Almighty. I will say of the Lord, 'He is my refuge and my fortress, my God, in whom I trust.' Surely He will save you from the Fowler's snare and from the deadly pestilence. He will cover you with His feathers, and under His wings you will find refuge; His faithfulness will be your shield and rampart."

Relationships are two-way

Every relationship is two-way. It is a give-and-take on both sides, or it just simply will not work but if you never talk to or show any emotion to the friend or love in your life, your relationship with them will not last very long. You cannot expect God to do everything! He already did it! He died for us! You want people to know what you think and feel and what you want and like, so you speak; you tell them. Well, God speaks through His word. To know what is important to God and how He wants to be worshiped and loved you must read His Word. The Bible is the written Word of God as spoken to the prophets through the Holy Spirit. Jesus is the living Word.

John 1:1-2 "In the beginning was the Word, and the Word was with God, and the Word was God. He was with God in the beginning."

Romans 5:8 "But God demonstrates His own love for us in this: While we were still sinners, Christ died for us."

2 Timothy 3:16-17 "All Scripture is God-breathed and is useful for teaching, rebuking, correcting and training in righteousness, so that the man of God may be thoroughly equipped for every good work."

God speaks to us in our hearts, but He speaks to us through His Word as well. As you read the Bible there will be a verse that almost jumps off the page at you! You will feel a quickening, a tug deep down in your heart and you will know that God is speaking to you through that verse; especially since it will be a verse pertaining to something that you are going through.

Job 4:12 "A word was secretly brought to me; my ears caught a whisper of it."

Job 33:14-16 "For God does speak—now one way, now another—though man may not perceive it. In a dream, in a vision of the night, when deep sleep falls on men as they slumber in their beds, He may speak in their ears and terrify them with warnings, to turn man from wrongdoing and keep him from pride, to preserve his soul from the pit, his life from perishing by the sword."

2 Peter 1:20-21 "Above all, you must understand that no prophecy of Scripture came about by the prophet's own interpretation. For prophecy never had its origin in the will of man, but men spoke from God as they were carried along by the Holy Spirit."

2 Samuel 23:2 "The Spirit of the Lord spoke through me; His Word was on my tongue."

John 14:26 "But the Counselor, the Holy Spirit, whom the Father will send in My name, will teach you all things and will remind you of everything I have said to you."

John 16:13 "But when He, the Spirit of truth comes, He will guide you into all truth. He will not speak on His own; He will speak only what He hears, and He will tell you what is yet to come."

The Word of God is our strength. Jesus is the Word who became flesh. He is our "bread of life," in which we find nourishment for our souls and our eternal salvation. He will meet all of your needs whether they are spiritual, physical, or emotional. You must let Him and trust Him to meet those needs. He died for your freedom. This is freedom from the chains that bind your heart. He will give you peace if you not only let Him in your heart but also have it and deal with the issues in it as well.

John 1:14 "The Word became flesh and made His dwelling among us. We have seen His glory, the glory of the One and Only who came from the Father, full of grace and truth."

John 6:47-48 "I tell you the truth; he who believes has everlasting life. I am the bread of life."

Psalm 29:11 "The Lord gives strength to His people; the Lord blesses His people with peace."

John 14:27 "Peace I leave with you; my peace I give you. I do not give to you as the world gives. Do not let your hearts be troubled and do not be afraid."

Isaiah 26:3 "You will keep in perfect peace him whose mind is steadfast, because he trusts in you."

By the blood of Jesus Christ, as we rely on and trust in Him, the grace of God will make you strong and help you to endure whatever it is that you are going through. Pray the Word and stand on it. Then trust God to answer or give you the Word that you are searching for and wait for Him to deliver it in His time. He knows best as you do for your own children. Everything has its own timing. A cake taken out of the oven too soon will fall. Trust in God. If you will only believe in the power of Jesus and open up to Him, He can and will bring victory to your defeats.

2 Corinthians 12:9-10 "My grace is sufficient for you, for my power is made perfect in weakness. Therefore I will boast all the more gladly about my weaknesses, so that Christ's power may rest on me. That is why, for Christ's sake, I delight in weaknesses, in insults, in hardships, in persecutions, in difficulties. For when I am weak, then I am strong."

Ecclesiastes 3:1 "There is a time for everything and a season for every activity under heaven."

Ecclesiastes 8:6 "For there is a proper time and procedure for every matter, though a man's misery weighs heavily upon him."

Romans 8:28 "And we know that in all things God works for the good of those who love Him, who have been called according to His purpose."

Psalm 138:2 "For You have exalted above all things Your name and Your Word."

Isaiah 7:9 "If you do not stand firm in your faith, you will not stand at all."

2 Thessalonians 2:15 "So then, brothers, stand firm and hold to the teachings we passed on to you, whether by word of mouth or by letter."

Faith comes by hearing the Word. God's Word that you receive by reading it and going to church regularly and Bible study. Remember, give and it will be given to you. Well, when you give to God, whether it is time, possessions, or money, you get so much more from Him than you could ever give of yourself. In order to get the Word deep down into your heart, soul, and mind so it will become real and alive to you, you must read it! Doing this will transform your mind into agreement with the will of God. As you do this, it changes the attitude of your heart and mind. When this happens, so does your actions. You start to grow spiritually.

Romans 10:17 "So then faith comes by hearing, and hearing by the Word of God."

Joshua 1:8 "Do not let this Book of the Law depart from your mouth; meditate on it day and night, so that you may be careful to do everything written in it. Then you will be prosperous and successful."

Romans 12:2 "Do not conform any longer to the patterns of this world but be transformed by the renewing of your mind. Then you will be able to test and approve what God's will is - His good, pleasing, and perfect will."

The Bible will not automatically become a wealth of knowledge in our minds upon conversion. Where it was hard to understand before, you will now understand it, but you have to read the Bible to understand it.

Psalm 146:7-8 "The Lord sets prisoners free; the Lord gives sight to the blind."

Proverbs 1:7 "The fear of the Lord is the beginning of knowledge."

Isaiah 6:9-10 "Be ever hearing, but never understanding; be ever seeing, but never perceiving. Make the heart of these people calloused; make their ears dull and close their eyes. Otherwise, they might see with their eyes, hear with their ears, understand with their hearts, and turn and be healed."

As you read the Bible, you are changed. The Words of God are life, whether they are from His written or spoken word. Reading the Bible and talking to the Lord daily along with regular church attendance and fellowship will help you to grow and mature and stay strong with a learning attitude as you go through trials. Trials are to help you learn and grow. Even Jesus was tested. Growing up you know that you truly learned right from wrong when you did something wrong and were punished. It sure became embedded in your spirit. You didn't want to be punished again so, even if it took a couple of times, you learned. You will also learn about yourself, where you fall short, and where you have progressed as the Lord does some gardening in your heart through trials and speaking to you through His Word.

James 1:2-5 "Consider it pure joy, my brothers, whenever you face trials of many kinds because you know that the testing of your faith develops perseverance. Perseverance must finish its work so that you may be mature and complete, not lacking anything. If any of you lacks wisdom, he should ask God, who gives generously to all without finding fault, and it will be given to him."

John 6:63 "The Spirit gives life; the flesh counts for nothing. The words I have spoken to you are spirit and they are life."

Matthew 4:1 "Then Jesus was led by the Spirit into the desert to be tempted by the devil."

Hebrews 2:17-18 "For this reason He had to be made like His brothers in every way, in order that He might become a merciful and faithful High Priest in service to God, and that He might make atonement for the sins of the people. Because He Himself suffered when He was tempted, He is able to help those who are being tempted."

Matthew 15:13 "Every plant that My heavenly Father has not planted will be pulled up by the roots."

Deuteronomy 7:22 " The Lord your God will drive out those nations before you, little by little. You will not be allowed to eliminate them all at once, or the wild animals will multiply around you."

John 17:17-19 "Sanctify them by the truth; your Word is truth. As you sent Me into the world, I have sent them into the world. For them, I sanctify Myself, that they too may be truly sanctified."

Psalm 119:105 "Your Word is a lamp to my feet and a light for my path."

In school, did your teachers give you all the answers and leave out the reading assignments, quizzes, and tests? No! That is how you learn. So, it is with your spiritual growth in Christ. As you read the Word and go through trials you grow as a Christian and are sanctified day-by-day, trial-by-trial. Your heart is being purified through it all. You have been given the Spirit of Jesus at conversion and the fruit of His Spirit, but it has to grow within you. You have years of the world in you that need to be purified and that are done through trials. As you go through trials, your spiritual growth process; the Word that you continually read is part of that process. It is planted in your heart as a seed. Everything is planted in you as a seed, seed, time, and harvest. The fullness of God dwells in Christ and the fullness of Christ dwells in us; the more time you spend with God in the Word the more of a harvest you will receive; a harvest of hearing the voice of God.

Mark 4:26-29 "This is what the kingdom of God is like; a man scatters seed on the ground. Night and day whether he sleeps or gets up, the seed sprouts and grows, though he does not know how. All by itself the soil produces grain-first the stalk, then the head, then the full kernel in the head. As soon as the grain is ripe, he puts the sickle to it, because the harvest has come."

Your growth is a process, not overnight.

Colossians 2:9-10 "For in Christ all the fullness of the Deity lives in bodily form, and you have been given fullness in Christ, who is the head over every power and authority."

Job 23:10 "But He knows the way that I take; when He has tested me, I will come forth as gold."

Psalm 51:10-12 "Create in me a pure heart, O God, and renew a steadfast spirit within me. Do not cast me from your presence or take Your Holy Spirit from me. Restore to me the joy of your salvation and grant me a willing spirit, to sustain me."

Colossians 2:20 "Since you died to the basic principles of this world, why, as though you still belonged to it, do you submit to its rules?"

1 Thessalonians 5:23 "May God Himself, the God of peace, sanctify you through and through?"

Galatians 4:6-7 "Because you are sons, God sent the Spirit of His Son into our hearts, the Spirit who calls out, "Abba, Father.' So, you are no longer a slave, but a son; and since you are a son, God has made you also an heir."

Galatians 5:22-23 "But the fruit of the Spirit is love, joy, peace, patience, kindness, goodness, faithfulness, gentleness and self-control."

1 Peter 1: 6-9 "In this you greatly rejoice, though now for a little while you may have had to suffer grief in all kinds of trials. These have come so that your faith - of greater worth than gold, which perishes even though refined by fire - may be proved genuine and may result in praise, glory, and honor when Jesus Christ is revealed. Though you have not seen Him, you love Him; and even though you do not see Him now, you believe in Him and are filled with an inexpressible and glorious joy, for you are receiving the goal of your faith, the salvation of your souls."

In preparing for a tough exam in school, especially semester exams you need to study. Should you not study the Word of God to live a life in the will and blessings of God? Is it not important enough for you to devote a little study time? After all, it came from God.

Psalm 1:1-3 "Blessed is the man who does not walk in the counsel of the wicked or stand in the way of sinners or sit in the seat of mockers. But his delight is in the law of the Lord, and on His law he meditates day and night. He is like a tree planted by streams of water, which yields its fruit in season and whose leaf does not wither. Whatever he does prospers."

John 1:1-2 "In the beginning was the Word, and the Word was with God, and the Word was God. He was with God in the beginning."

The one and only Creator of heaven and earth, the One who saves, restores, heals, and blesses you, does He not deserve a little time out of your day; time just to be in His awesome, peace-giving wonderful presence? Time talking to Him as you would talk to your closest friend; after all, He is the best friend that you will ever have. Time reading His Word is also time in His presence.

Proverbs 18:24 "A man of many companions may come to ruin, but there is a friend who sticks closer than a brother."

Deuteronomy 4:39-40 "Acknowledge and take to heart this day that the Lord is God in heaven above and on the earth below. There is no other. Keep His decrees and commands, which I am giving you today, so that it may go well with you and your children after you and that you may live long in the land the Lord your God gives you for all time."

Psalm 67:5-7 "May the peoples praise You, O God; may all the peoples praise you. Then the land will yield its harvest, and God, our God, will bless us. God will bless us, and all the ends of the earth will fear Him."

Psalm 68:19-20 "Praise be to the Lord, to God our Savior, who daily bears our burdens. Our God is a God who saves; from the Sovereign Lord comes escape from death."

There is so much to the Bible that you just cannot get all you need out of it by just reading it alone. In most Scriptures, there are several meanings. Verses that have symbolism to it that as you trust God to teach you, He will. There will be meanings for that particular time, a prophecy for the future, and an application for your everyday life. Even David prayed to God to show him His ways and to teach him.

Psalm 25:4-5 "Show me your ways, O Lord, teach me your paths; guide me in your truth and teach me, for you are God my Savior, and my hope is in you all day long."

Psalm 143:8-10 "Let the morning bring me word of your unfailing love, for I have put my trust in you. Show me the way I should go, for to you I lift up my soul. Rescue me from my enemies, O Lord, for I hide myself in you. Teach me to do your will, for you are my God; may your good Spirit lead me on level ground."

Daniel 2:21-22 "He gives wisdom to the wise and knowledge to the discerning. He reveals deep and hidden things; He knows what lies in darkness, and light dwells with Him."

The Word of God is a double-edged sword.

The word of God is living and active. It is a double-edged sword penetrating your soul and helping you to grow while convicting others that they are a sinner and need a Savior, Jesus Christ. As you stay in the Word and draw closer to God, He will draw closer to God, make everything clear, and straighten your paths before you.

Hebrews 4:12 "For the Word of God is living and active. Sharper than any double-edged sword, it penetrates even to dividing soul and spirit, joints and marrow; it judges the thoughts and attitudes of the heart."

James 4:7-8 "Submit yourselves, then, to God. Resist the devil, and he will flee from you. Come near to God and He will come near to you."

John 16:8 "When He comes, He will convict the world of guilt in regard to sin and righteousness and judgment."

Proverbs 3:5-6 "Trust in the Lord with all your heart and lean not on your own understanding; in all your ways acknowledge Him, and He will make your paths straight."

Luke 3:5 "Every valley shall be filled in, every mountain and hill made low. The crooked roads shall become straight, the rough ways smooth."

Studying the Word will help you to examine yourself and see yourself as God sees you. After all, wouldn't you rather see the sin in your life through the Word of God rather than through trials? I know I would. I have enough trials and I do not want any more than I have to go through. One way or another as any good parent, God will teach you, as a child of God, His ways and the path that He wants you on. Doing His will brings blessings, rebelling, and being disobedient brings discipline and wrath.

2 Corinthians 13:5 "Examine yourselves to see whether you are in the faith; test yourselves."

Ephesians 5:7 "God's wrath comes on those who are disobedient."

Hebrews 12:5-7 "My son, do not make light of the Lord's discipline and do not lose heart when he rebukes you, because the Lord disciplines those he loves, and he punishes everyone he accepts as a son. Endure hardship as discipline; God is treating you as sons."

1 Samuel 15:23 "To obey is better than sacrifice, and to heed is better than the fat of rams. For rebellion is like the sin of divination, and arrogance like the evil of idolatry."

Deuteronomy 30:19-20 "This day I call heaven and earth as witnesses against you that I have set before you life and death, blessings and curses. Now choose life, so that you and your children may live and that you may love the Lord your God, listen to His voice, and hold fast to Him. For the Lord is your life, and He will give you many years in the land He swore to give to your fathers, Abraham, Isaac, and Jacob."

As we study the Word, talk to Him daily, and attend church regularly you will have the strength to endure through your trials. You will have what you need, supplied by God, through His Word, through your Pastor or other Christians sent to you by God to encourage you. Stay close to Him and stay in His Word and when you need a word, you will have one. You also become more and more like Jesus Christ through it all. Isn't that our goal?

2 Corinthians 3:17-18 "Now the Lord is the Spirit, and where the Spirit of the Lord is, there is freedom. And we, who with unveiled faces all reflect the Lord's glory, are being transformed into His likeness with ever-increasing glory, which comes from the Lord, who is the Spirit."

Praying Effectively

There are several things needed to pray effectively. God wants us to pray. This is our way of communicating with God, not just in asking for something but as a way of being intimate with Him and getting to know Him.

Luke 18:1 "Then Jesus told His disciples a parable to show them that they should always pray and not give up."

1 Thessalonians 5:16-18 "Be joyful always; pray continually; give thanks in all circumstances, for this is God's will for you in Christ Jesus."

1 Timothy 2:1-4 "I urge, then, first of all, that requests, prayers, intercession, and thanksgiving be made for everyone - for kings and all those in authority, that we may live peaceful and quiet lives in all godliness and holiness. This is good and pleases God our Savior, who wants all men to be saved and to come to a knowledge of the truth."

According to Dr. Myles Munroe (Keys for Prayer), prayer is also: an "Earthly license for heavenly interference." (Page 8, 2008) God gave man dominion over the earth. Since God exalts His name and His word above all things, He too must abide by His word so that we may trust Him and His word. He gave man free will, so in order for God to act, we must ask. This is why we must pray!!!! Prayer is also the prevention of sin, not the antidote. Prayer is a sin killer. Don't wait until sin has overtaken you to pray. Pray before when you are being tempted. God will provide a way of escape. God hears and knows our hearts. So, be sincere, not phony- He does not want lip service.

1 Corinthians 10:12-13 "So, if you think you are standing firm, be careful that you don't fall! No temptation has seized you except what is common to man. And God is faithful; He will not let you be tempted beyond what you can bear. But when you are tempted, He will also provide a way out so that you can stand up under it."

Genesis 1:26 "Let us make man in Our image, in Our likeness, and let them rule over the fish of the sea and the birds of the air, over the livestock, over all the earth, and over all the creatures that move along the ground."

Hebrews 10:22 "Let us draw near to God with a sincere heart in full assurance of faith, having our hearts sprinkled to cleanse us from a guilty conscience and having our bodies washed with pure water."

Pray effectively

1. Be a child of God

In order for your Heavenly Father to answer your prayers He must first be your Father.

John 1:12 "Yet to all who received Him, to those who believe in His name, He gave the right to become children of God."

James 1:18 "He chose to give us birth through the word of truth that we might be a kind of first fruits of all He created."

2. Be in the right standing with God

We will all go through a growing stage as we mature as Christians, and we are sanctified daily. Just as you grow from a baby into an adult and you make mistakes along the way as you learn right from wrong, so it is in your Christian growth.

Romans 3:23 "For all have sinned and fall short of the glory of God."

Psalm 34:15 "The eyes of the Lord are on the righteous and His ears are attentive to their cry."

Proverbs 28:9 "If anyone turns a deaf ear to the law, even his prayers are detestable."

John 9:31 "We know that God does not listen to sinners. He listens to the godly man who does His will."

Thanks be to God for His abounding love, mercy, grace, and forgiveness. He has already provided for our growth and sanctification process. He knows that we will fall short and sin from time to time. He doesn't like it, but He knows the sin nature within us. That provision is the saving grace provided through our Lord and Savior Jesus Christ.

John 1:9 "If we confess our sins, He is faithful and just and will forgive us our sins and purify us from all unrighteousness."

We must come before God with a pure heart. He is holy. Pray to God daily for this, to purify your heart and open your eyes to the sins you are not aware of.

Psalm 51:10 "Create in me a pure heart, O God, and renew a steadfast spirit within me."

Isaiah 52:11 "Depart, depart, and go out from there! Touch no unclean thing! Come out from it and be pure, you who carry the vessels of the Lord."

2 Chronicles 7:14 "If My people, who are called by My name, will humble themselves and pray and seek My face and turn from their wicked ways, then will I hear from heaven and will forgive their sin and will heal their land."

3. Confess

If you have any offense or unforgiveness in your heart you must confess it and forgive sincerely just as God forgave you. In not forgiving, you are placing yourself above Jesus, the one who died for your sins!

Mark 11:25-26 "And when you stand praying, if you hold anything against anyone, forgive him, so that your Father in heaven may forgive you your sins."

4. Pray in the name of Jesus

As He breathed His last the veil of the Temple curtain was torn. This symbolized our access to the Father through Jesus Christ. He paid the price for our sins and as we receive Him into our hearts as Lord and Savior, we now have access to the Father through Him.

John 16:23-24 "I tell you the truth, My Father will give you whatever you ask in my name. Until now you have not asked for anything in my name. Ask and you will receive, and your joy will be complete."

5. Believe

If you do not come believing, then why do you come at all?

Hebrews 11:6 "And without faith it is impossible to please God, because anyone who comes to Him must believe that He exists and that He rewards those who earnestly seek Him."

James 1:6-7 "But when he asks, he must believe and not doubt, because he who doubts is like a wave of the sea, blown and tossed by the wind. That man should not think he will receive anything from the Lord."

Matthew 21:22 "If you believe, you will receive whatever you ask for in prayer."

6. Have the right motives

God knows your heart.   You cannot sugarcoat anything you are praying for to make it look like it is for a good cause if indeed it is prayed with selfish motives.

James 4:3 "When you ask, you do not receive, because you ask with wrong motives, that you may spend what you get on your pleasures."

Proverbs 16:2 "All a man's ways seem innocent to him, but motives are weighed by the Lord."

7. Pray the Word

This is one of the most effective ways of praying. There are Scriptures in the Bible for every circumstance. To do this you must be familiar with the Word and that means reading the Bible. Something we are all called to do, this is our strength against   Satan, and it transforms our minds to the will of God. Our hearts were transformed at conversion, but our minds have had years of the world packed into it and that takes time through trials, which sanctifies us and through reading the Word of God. Pray the Word and speak it; you give birth to whatever you speak.

Proverbs 18:21 "The tongue has the power of life and death, and those who love it will eat its fruit."

Psalm 138:2 "For you have exalted above all things your name and Your Word."

Romans 12:2 "Do not conform any longer to the patterns of this world, but be transformed by the renewing of your mind."

Joshua 1:8 "Do not let this Book of the Law depart from your mouth; meditate on it day and night, so that you may be careful to do everything written in it. Then you will be prosperous and successful."

2 Corinthians 5:17 "Therefore, if anyone is in Christ, He is a new creation."

You have His Holy Spirit within you, but your mind is still the same. It is your heart that has changed. Your mind needs to be renewed day by day.

Ephesians 4:22-24 "You were taught, with regard to your former way of life, to put off your old self, which is being corrupted by its deceitful desires; to be made new in the attitude of your minds; and to put on the new self, created to be like God in true righteousness and holiness."

8. What to pray
If you are not sure how to pray, cast it on Jesus. Ask Him to intercede on your behalf.

Psalm 55:22 "Cast your cares on the Lord and He will sustain you; He will never let the righteous fall."

9. Talk to God
You must pray to talk to God and not just to come asking for something all the time. You cannot have just a 'give me' relationship with God. That is selfishness which is a sin and will hinder your prayers from being answered. In any relationship, if you are taking all the time and not giving, your relationship will suffer. God wants to be loved by you. He created you in His image, therefore the emotions He gave you, He had first. If you need to be loved and praised and thanked and appreciated, so does God.

Psalm 144:3 "O Lord, what is man that you care for him, the son of man that you think of him?"

Psalm 145:13 "The Lord is faithful to all His promises and loving toward all He has made."

John 4:16 "God is Love".

John 4: 19 "We love because He first loved us."

He loved us when He created us; to be His children.

Jeremiah 31:3 "I have loved you with an everlasting love; I have drawn you with loving-kindness."

James 4:7-8 "Submit yourselves, then, to God. Resist the devil, and he will flee from you. Come near to God and He will come near to you."

Psalm 73:28 "But as for me, it is good to be near God. I have made the Sovereign Lord my refuge; I will tell of all your deeds."

Jeremiah 29:11-14 "For I know the plans I have for you, declares the Lord, plans to prosper you and not to harm you, plans to give you hope and a future. Then you will call upon Me and come and pray to Me, and I will listen to you. You will seek Me and find Me when you seek Me with all your heart. I will be found by you, declares the Lord, and bring you back from captivity."

10. Worship and praise God

He is your Creator, He is your God, He is your Lord and Savior, He is Your Provider, He is your healer, He is your joy, He is the love within your heart, He is your Victory, He is your peace, He is the One who sanctifies you, He is your Righteousness, He is your Shepherd who is always with you, He is your Guide, He is your protector and He is your Refuge and Strength! This alone is more than enough to praise His holy name! Praise Him and love Him and obey Him for who He is! Your needs will be taken care of, and your prayers will be answered! He is God Almighty and He already knows your needs!

Matthew 6:8 "Your Father knows what you need before you ask Him."

Matthew 4:10 "Worship the Lord your God, and serve Him only."

John 4:24 "God is Spirit, and His worshipers must worship in spirit and in truth."

Psalm 100:2 "Worship the Lord with gladness; come before Him with joyful songs."

Most people have someone they are praying for who is lost and needs to make Jesus the Lord of their life.

Scripture references on the salvation of lost loved ones:

1 Thessalonians 5:9-10
Acts 16:31
1 Peter 3:9

Do not get discouraged. God never promised immediate answers and Satan will try and discourage you and make you lose hope. DON'T FALL FOR HIS LIES! God says He is faithful and He will answer your prayers! The people you are praying for must do the asking, but God knows their heart. He created it. He also knows that a special knock on the door that will cause them to open it and let Him in. You must only keep trusting, praying, and obeying God. Victory is yours! He promised!

1 Corinthians 15:54-57 "Death has been swallowed up in victory. Where, O death, is your victory? Where, O death, is your sting? The sting of death is sin, and the power of sin is the law. But thanks be to God! He gives us the victory through our Lord Jesus Christ."

Psalm 60:12 "With God we will gain the victory, and He will trample down our enemies."

Prayer is the wiring that connects to God's power and love.

1. Prayer kills the sin from a burdened heart
2. Prayer is a power breaker - it breaks strongholds
3. The power of prayer convicts and heals the lost and backslidden
4. Prayer is an anxiety healer
5. Prayer is a conversation with God
6. Prayer draws us closer to God

People of prayer

1. Are powerful
2. Have God's presence
3. Have God's provision
4. Have God's promises

Pray over these for yourself:

When you ask God for these virtues, you are asking God to transform you into the very image of Christ.
Psalm 119:116-117, 132-135

1. Love
2. Joy
3. Peace
4. Patience
5. Kindness
6. Goodness
7. Faithfulness
8. Gentleness
9. Self-Control

Foundations Of A Powerful Prayer Life

The 3 Foundations

Foundation 1

You must view your daily prayer time as a (love) relationship with God and not some legalistic duty or discipline (2 Chronicles 7:14).

Foundation 2

You must make an absolute commitment to consistently spend time alone with God in uninterrupted prayer. This shows spiritual maturity (Matt. 6:6), (Ephesians 6:10-17).

Foundation 3

A powerful prayer life requires the "balanced practice" of all five types of prayer:

1. Praise, thanksgiving, and worship
2. Confession and repentance
3. Petition and supplication
4. Intercession
5. Meditation

Prayer must be a balanced practice of all five types of prayer. You need balanced meals from all the food groups and the same is true with prayer.

If you have never read the Bible and just beginning; start reading in the Book of John.

Read God's Word every day because you are the only Bible that a lot of people will ever read. We are God's hands, feet, voice, and His arms in the world. You are the temple of God. You are His representative in the world.

You need sincere love, zeal to serve and a humble heart as you seek a closer relationship with God. Prayer is vital for this.

The vitality of prayer

1. Prayer is your love and trust in God and coming to   Him to want to know Him more.
2. Serving God - attending to God's needs- Jesus came for ours- worship and praise God, pray- talk to Him every day and do what He calls you to do.
3. Prayer time - is planned time; significant times set aside in a solitary place and bring your Bible. If Jesus, the son of God spent much time in prayer then why shouldn't we? (Mark 4:35). We will not reach spiritual maturity unless we do.

What Has You Paralyzed?

Matthew 9:1-8 "Jesus stepped into a boat; crossed over and came to His own town. Some men brought to him a paralytic, lying on a mat. When Jesus saw their faith, He said to the paralytic, 'Take heart, son; your sins are forgiven.'"

At this, some of the teachers of the law said to themselves, "This fellow is blaspheming!"

Knowing their thoughts, Jesus said, "Why do you entertain evil thoughts in your hearts? Which is easier: to say, 'Your sins are forgiven,' or to say, 'Get up and walk?' But so that you may know that the Son of Man has authority on earth to forgive sins...." Then He said to the paralytic, "Get up, take your mat, and go home." And the man got up and went home. When the crowd saw this, they were filled with awe; and they praised God, who had given such authority to men."

Identify the problem

When in your heart and mind an inner battle is going on - you are imprisoned, feet chained. You are paralyzed, immobile, and not able to grow in the Lord or be freed from the battle within.

Acts 16:24 "Upon receiving such orders, he put them in the inner cell and fastened their feet in the stocks."

What sin, the act of defiance, or downright disobedience, what area of doubt has you bound, paralyzed, or stuck? You are in a place in life you cannot seem to get out of; you want to change, but you cannot seem to get anywhere or make it happen. Being paralyzed is not just physical.

It can be an emotional state of being as well. Regardless of the reason, both will paralyze you and stunt your spiritual growth.

Something you might be doing:

Maybe what you are doing did not start out as disobedience; you just needed an escape, and issues were getting to you. You could not help it, but deep inside you knew it was wrong and just could not stop. The Lord is there to help, and His understanding and mercy are beyond measure. "Great is our Lord and mighty in power; His understanding has no limit" (Psalm 147:5). Humble yourself before Him and cry out to Him. "Submit yourselves, then, to God. Resist the devil, and he will flee from you. Come near to God and He will come near to you. Wash your hands, you sinners, and purify your hearts, you double-minded. Grieve, mourn, and wail. Change your laughter to mourning and your joy to gloom. Humble yourselves before the Lord, and He will lift you up," (James 4:7-10).

Emotional issues:

Maybe you are not doing anything; you are the one who has been hurt so bad it has left you depressed and brokenhearted. The depression is so dark; that you don't want to do anything. It has left you lifeless. You have no strength to pull yourself up, but deep inside you want it. Deep inside your heart is screaming. Cry out to the Lord, He hears your cry. "He heals the brokenhearted and binds up their wounds," (Psalm 147:3).

What do you do?

Examine your motives; search your heart and go to the Lord in prayer. Ask Him if you just do not know.

Lamentation 3:40 "Let us examine our ways and test them and let us return to the Lord."

Proverbs 16:2 "All a man's ways seem innocent to him, but motives are weighed by the Lord."

Proverbs 21:2 "All a man's ways seem right to him, but the Lord weighs the heart."

The man in the story had friends and they brought him to Jesus. If you truly want change; to get out of depression, to believe, or to break the bad habits you have created while in your "wilderness" period that have become harmful to you, your loved ones, and your spiritual growth you must do something. In John chapter 5 there was a man who was lame, paralyzed for 38 years. In Jerusalem near the Sheep Gate, there was a pool, and the lame would gather there and when the waters were stirred by the Spirit of the Lord they would get in, in hopes of being healed. When Jesus came to this man and saw him lying beside it, He asked him "Do you want to get well?" The man replied, "I have no one to help me into the pool when the water is stirred." If you truly want to get out of the box you are in you will find the strength to call on the Lord. He is always there and wants to help you. He will put people in your path or tell you or do something to get your attention, but if you do not see Him trying to get your attention, you may have to learn the hard way, when you just can't take it anymore. He is "gentle and humble in heart" and will not force Himself on you, but He longs to bless you and help you to grow. Satan does not want the children of the Lord to grow spiritually; because when we do, we are being active in our faith! That means more people are being witnessed to and more people are being saved! He does not want that! It is really a battle between Satan and God. Here are some steps to take:

Know who the battle belongs to

The battle belongs to the Lord. "Do not be afraid or discouraged because of this vast army. For the battle is not yours, but God's." (2 Chronicles 20:15). - Go to the Lord in prayer. He is your heavenly Father and He loves you!

Seek out a Christian friend.

The Lord comforts us when we are down; He understands. He has been there, remember the Garden the night He was betrayed? He was very troubled in spirit "His sweat was as drops of blood." (Luke 22:44) "Praise be to the God and Father of our Lord Jesus Christ, the Father of compassion and the God of all comfort who comforts us in all our troubles, so that we can comfort those in any trouble with the comfort we ourselves have received from God. For just as the sufferings of Christ flow over into our lives, so also through Christ our comfort overflows. If we are distressed, it is for our comfort and salvation; if we are comforted, it is for your comfort, which produces in you patient endurance of the same sufferings we suffer. And our hope for you is firm because we know that just as you share in our sufferings, so also you share in our comfort." (2 Corinthians 1:3-7). Your true Christian friends will be there to help encourage you, comfort you, and give you wisdom from the Lord.

Seek council from your Pastor.

Have your Pastor or a member of your Church's prayer team pray for you. Your Pastor is a shepherd, and it is His calling to serve the Lord not only in preaching a sermon but to give council, guidance, discipleship, and correction where needed.

Be sincere

You must come to the Lord with a sincere heart. The Lord knows your heart. "Let us draw near to God with a sincere heart in full assurance of faith, having our hearts sprinkled to cleanse us from a guilty conscience and having our bodies washed with pure water" (Hebrews 10:22). It will not do you any good if you cannot own up to the problem you have; without admitting to yourself that you have a problem then you will not truly have the will to change. If you want something different then you must do something different. You cannot keep doing the same thing and expect to get a different outcome. You cannot keep planting apple seeds and expect an orange tree to grow. If you are not sincere with yourself, you will stay in the pit you are in. If you are sitting "on the fence" - you want to change but still doubt, still have those urges or cravings for the things that have you bound, tell that to the Lord. He can work with that because you are being honest. He cannot work with a lie. "God is spirit, and His worshipers must worship Him in spirit and in truth." (John 4:24). Ask God to give you an undivided heart.

Confess

If you have traveled down a road of addiction or some other way of life that you know is wrong, humble yourself and confess. Come back to the Lord and He will help you to get back on "the straight and narrow path" once again. "But if we walk in the light, as He is in the light, we have fellowship with one another, and the blood of Jesus, His Son, purifies us from all sin. If we claim to be without sin, we deceive ourselves and the truth is not in us. If we confess our sins, He is faithful and just and will forgive us our sins and purify us from all unrighteousness" (John 1:7-9).

Trust God to turn things around.

Faith and hope in God is the tree of life. It is the strength you need to make it through because you already know the outcome; you win! "The Lord gives strength to His people; the Lord blesses His people with peace," (Psalm 29:11). When you have hope then you will believe. "Abraham in hope believed." (Romans 4:18) "The Lord is faithful to all His promises and loving toward all He has made," (Psalm 145:13). God will fulfill all the promises He made you.

(Lamentations 3:22-23) "Because of the Lord's great love we are not consumed, for His compassion's never fail. They are new every morning; great is your faithfulness."

Don't throw away your confidence!

You have now made a step in the right direction and Satan is not going to sit idly by and let that happen. "So do not throw away your confidence; it will be richly rewarded. You need to persevere so that when you have done the will of God, you will receive what he has promised. For in just a very little while, He who is coming will come and will not delay. But my righteous one will live by faith. And if he shrinks back, I will not be pleased with him. But we are not of those who shrink back and are destroyed, but of those who believe and are saved." (Hebrews 10:35-39). He will try to shoot one of his fiery darts at you with some sort of trouble to keep you down. Don't fall for it! Your new-found hope in Christ again has brought you the peace and joy of Christ! Don't let Satan steal it. "The thief comes only to steal and kill and destroy; I have come that they may have life and have it to the full." (John 10:10).

Keep praising God

King Jehoshaphat, in 2 Chronicles 20, had 3 large armies coming up against the people of Judah and Jerusalem. On their own they were helpless. Jehoshaphat admitted their weakness to the Lord and the fact that He did not know what to do. He went before the Lord and told Him. The Lord told him to go out before the armies and face them. In other words, sitting back and wallowing in self-pity will get you nowhere. Trusting in God will win the battle for you. "With God, we will gain the victory, and He will trample down our enemies," (Psalm 60:12). God told him that the battle was not theirs; it was HIS. They went out into battle the next day and instead of taking their fighting stance, they took on one of praise. They started singing to the Lord.

"Or yet you are holy, enthroned on the praises of Israel" (Psalm 22:3).
In other words, God is right there in the middle of your praises, and if
God is for us who can be against us?

Conclusion

1. Keep going to Church

You never know when God will speak a word to you through the Pastor's sermon or even the Word of God he is reading that day.

2. Pray and get Prayer

Have someone pray for you. He says in James 4:2 "You do not have because you do not ask God."

3. Admit your sin or doubt

"God opposes the proud but gives grace to the humble," (James 4:6).

4. Ask for His help to overcome strongholds

In Mark 9 a father asking for healing for his son believed yet had some doubt as well. He admitted it to the Lord. "I do believe; help me overcome my unbelief!" (Mark 9:24). The Lord healed his son.

5. Ask for forgiveness

If we sincerely confess our sins He will forgive us. "For I will forgive their wickedness and will remember their sins no more," (Hebrews 8:12).

6. Give Him praise

Everyone likes to be loved and appreciated. It hurts you when your children do not believe you; so, it is with God. "May the peoples praise You, O God; may all the peoples praise you. Then the land will yield its harvest, and God, our God, will bless us. God will bless us, and all the ends of the earth will fear Him," (Psalm 67:5-7).

7. Wait in Faith

Faith pleases God. "And without faith, it is impossible to please God, because anyone who comes to him must believe that he exists and that he rewards those who earnestly seek Him" (Hebrews 11:6). "I am still confident of this: I will see the goodness of the Lord in the land of the living. Wait for the Lord; be strong and take heart and wait for the Lord," (Psalm 27:13-14).

Praising and thanking God tells Him you love, trust, and appreciate Him. When depressing or fearful thoughts come, and something catches your eye and makes you laugh, the bad thoughts seem to disappear. Well, if you are praising God, Satan is not going to stick around and praise God with you! He is going to leave you alone! So, keep praising God! Our victory rests in God alone!

Revelation 12:10-11 "Then I heard a loud voice in heaven say: "Now have come the salvation and the power and the kingdom of our God and the authority of His Christ. For the accuser of our brothers, who accuses them before our God day and night, has been hurled down. They overcame him by the blood of the Lamb and by the word of their testimony; they did not love their lives so much as to shrink from death."

It will take time; you did not get where you are overnight but trust God; He will fulfill every promise and make your crooked paths straight.

Luke 3:4-6 "As is written in the book of the words of Isaiah the prophet: "A voice of one calling in the desert, 'Prepare the way for the Lord, make straight paths for Him. Every valley shall be filled in, every mountain and hill made low. The crooked roads shall become straight, the rough ways smooth. And all mankind will see God's salvation."

If you give God time, He will lift you up out of the pit you are in; a crop takes time to grow.

Psalm 40:1-2 "I waited patiently for the Lord; He turned to me and heard my cry. He lifted me out of the slimy pit, out of the mud and mire; He set my feet on a rock and gave me a firm place to stand."

In its season you will have a field to harvest if you water it. Water your faith through the reading of God's Word.

Romans 10:17 "Consequently faith comes by hearing and hearing the message and the message is heard through the word of Christ."

Follow the steps above and you will see a harvest of blessings come to pass.

Your victory is promised - just believe.

Zephaniah 3:14-20 "The remnant of Israel will do no wrong; they will speak no lies, nor will deceit be found in their mouths. They will eat and lie down, and no one will make them afraid. Sing, O Daughter of Zion; shout aloud, O Israel! Be glad and rejoice with all your heart, O Daughter of Jerusalem! The Lord has taken away your punishment; He has turned back your enemy. The Lord, the King of Israel, is with you; never again will you fear any harm. On that day they will say to Jerusalem, 'Do not fear, O Zion; do not let your hands hang limp. The Lord your God is with you, He is mighty to save. He will take great delight in you, He will quiet you with His love, He will rejoice over you with singing.' The sorrows for the appointed feasts I will remove from you; they are a burden and a reproach to you. At that time, I will deal with all who oppressed you; I will rescue the lame and gather those who have been scattered. I will give them praise and honor in every land where they were put to shame. At that time, I will gather you; at that time, I will bring you home. I will give you honor and praise among all the peoples of the earth when I restore your fortunes before your very eyes," says the Lord."

Will You Not Learn?

Jeremiah 35:13 "This is what the Lord Almighty, the God of Israel, says: Go and tell the people of Judah and those living in Jerusalem, 'Will you not learn a lesson and obey my words?' declares the Lord."

When you are sinning against the Lord; to draw you to Him, He will let bad things happen; to warn you to receive Jesus as Lord and Savior and to receive forgiveness and to change your ways and repent.

Job 33:29-30 "God does all these things to a man twice, even three times- to turn back his soul from the pit, that the light of life may shine on him."

Your continued sin will bring only destruction and God's wrath.

Jeremiah 2:17 "Have you not brought this on yourselves by forsaking God when He led you in the way?"

Jeremiah 2:19 "Your wickedness will punish you; your backsliding will rebuke you."

And still, you refuse to submit to God's will and go your own way.

Matthew 7:21 "Not everyone who says to Me Lord, Lord will enter the kingdom of heaven, but only he who does the will of My Father who is in heaven."

Without a true change of heart and obedience to God, his warnings and discipline will continue.

He asks, "Will you not learn a lesson and obey my words?" (Jeremiah 35:13)

His discipline and warnings may come in different forms; many caused by your own sin. You reap what you sow.

Galatians 6:7-8 "A man reaps what he sows. The one who reaps to please his sinful nature, from that nature will reap destruction; the one who sows to please the Spirit, from the Spirit will reap eternal life."

If you let the desires of the sinful nature rule your life, the lusts and addictions of the world, they become your idol or your god. An idol is anything you give excessive devotion or reverence to. That should only be God!

Exodus 20:3-4 "You shall have no other gods before me. You shall not make for yourself an idol in the form of anything in heaven above or on the earth beneath or in the waters below."

Physical addictions to anything will:

1. Ruin your health
2. Overtake- ruin your finances
3. Cause emotional problems
4. All of these problems will lead to:
5. Family problems

Emotional obsessions or problems will cause:

1. Depression and despair
2. Lack of energy- no desire to accomplish anything   laziness

3. Other lustful desires that begin to take priority in   your life
4. Instability
5. All of these lead to:
6. Financial difficulties
7. Family problems

Recognize the warnings from God and repent before it is too late! Be sincere, God knows your true heart. He knows sincerity from lip service!

Proverbs 21:2 "All a man's ways seem right to him, but the Lord weighs the heart."

Repent! God wants to bless you! He takes no pleasure in disciplining you.

Jeremiah 13:17 "But if you do not listen, I will weep in secret because of your pride; my eyes will weep bitterly, overflowing with tears, because the Lord's flock will be taken captive."

What is taking you captive? Give it to God, repent, and be blessed!

Jeremiah 32:40-41 "I will make an everlasting covenant with them: I will never stop doing good to them, and I will inspire them to fear me so that they will never turn away from me! I will rejoice in doing them good and will assuredly plant them in this land with all my heart and soul."

Do Not Worry - Trust God!

God commands in this passage 3x "Do not worry!" This is not just a command to not worry, but it is also a command to trust Him!

Reference passages:

Matthew 6:25-34 - This passage tells of how God takes care of the birds in the air and the lilies of the field. They are always taken care of, and He asks, is our life and are we not more valuable than they?

Matthew 6:7-8 - God knows what you need before you even ask.

Matthew 7:7-11 - He says ask and you shall receive.

Why We Worry

1. Worry is a result of a faith failure.

2. We don't know the Word of God; therefore, we are unaware of the promises in His Word for us. So, we are in conflict with God.

3. We listen to other people instead of going to God when advice from other people may be based on their feelings and opinions- for they are controlled by emotions just like you.

Consequences of Worry

1. You will end up in chronic bondage
2. It divides your mind.
3. Your emotions become fragmented.
4. It drains your energy. You no longer feel like doing anything and the things that you do is not at your best performance.
5. It clouds your thinking- you stay confused – you can't think straight.
6. You can't seem to make decisions.
7. You start having "pity parties"
8. You withdraw from other people, or you notice everyone else withdrawing from you. This is because you are always complaining. No one likes to be around someone who is always complaining and always depressed. More than likely, they have a lot of problems of their own and do not need yours to add to theirs.
9. You become angry and irritable.
10. You question God's love for you.
11. Your prayer life takes a nosedive.
12. Your health starts to deteriorate, you begin to get headaches, lose sleep, and get anxiety attacks. At this point do not go to your medicine cabinet alone to rid yourself of your headaches, get on your knees, and go to God in prayer. Ask Him to let you know what your problem is if you have not discovered it yet by this time. He will answer you. Too many people grab a pill for depression first before going to the Creator. God should always be your first cry for help! Crying out to God is free and it keeps you

from getting addicted to pills. He is God almighty and quite capable of helping you.

13. You find yourself in the center of materialism, thinking that things will make you feel better. This does not help. It only gets you in debt, which creates more worry.

14. You lose your testimony. The people who know that you are a Christian and see you with a look of depression will wonder how a Christian can be so unhappy when God is supposed to be taking care of them and keeping them in peace and joy.

Reasons why you do not need to worry

1. He knows what you need before you ask.
2. You are to store up treasures in heaven - Seek God first, and He will take care of the rest.
3. Our life is more important than material things. He created us, He can take care of us.
4. You are valuable to God.
5. He died for your salvation- Don't you think that He will take care of that which He died for?
6. Will worrying add 1 minute, hour, or day to your life? Will worrying fix your problem?
1. Worrying is a lack of faith.

Overcoming worry

1. Remember your Father knows and sees your need and is with you
   in your need.
2. View the problem in the context of your faith - from God's eyes
   according to the promises of His Word. Take your eyes off of the
   problem and put them on God.
3. Seek God's kingdom first. His kingdom means His rule or Lord-
   ship over your heart, soul, life, and mind, living daily life in obedience to God in Christ likeness and righteousness the blood of
   Jesus Christ.

CHAPTER 4

Spiritual Warfare: Standing Against The Devil

When the Israelites were about to enter into Canaan, the Lord told Moses to send out 12 spies to explore the land. This was not to see what they were up against to scare them, but to see for themselves the land they were about to enter. The Lord already told them that He would go with them and give the land to them. The purpose was so that they would be encouraged when they saw the goodness of what God was about to deliver into their hands and so that they could see the people who lived there for themselves.

In doing that they could develop a battle plan. They could not just charge in there without a battle plan. That is the reason we have the Bible; we explore history, we learn of God's goodness and His promises, and we learn how to obey God. We learn what pleases Him and what does not, and we also learn how to pray and how to be saved. We learn what the consequences of our actions are, and we also learn of the blessings we have as a child of God as well.

Lastly, we learn Scripture and how and when to use it and stand on it; we learn about the battle plan God has for us in living a victorious Christian life and defeating Satan! "All scripture is God-breathed and is useful for teaching, rebuking, correcting and training in righteousness, so that the man of God may be thoroughly equipped for every good work," (2 Timothy 3:16-17).

The Bible is our weapon; a gift from God; it is His written Word as if He was physically speaking to us.

"May the praise of God be in their mouths and a double-edged sword in their hands." (Psalm 149:6).

Stay in God's Word and fellowship, go to church regularly, and talk to God daily. This will keep you close to God and keep His strength and His power working strong in you to lead.

Deliverance: Overcoming Spiritual Warfare

Know what the battle really is

It is Spiritual warfare - Satan trying to destroy mankind and especially the children of God and their walk with Him.

Ephesians 6:12 "For our struggle is not against flesh and blood, but against the rulers, against the authorities, against the powers of this dark world and against the spiritual forces of evil in the heavenly realms."

1 Peter 5:8-10 "Be self-controlled and alert. Your enemy the devil prowls around like a roaring lion looking for someone to devour. Resist him, standing firm in the faith, because you know that your brothers throughout the world are undergoing the same kind of suffering. And the God of all grace, who called you to His eternal glory in Christ, after you have suffered a little while, will Himself restore you and make you strong, firm, and steadfast."

Know who the battle really belongs to

It belongs to God.

2 Chronicles 20:15 "For the battle is not yours, but God's."

Stand firm in your faith and you will be delivered.

Keep Scripture references handy to meditate on that pertain to your circumstances and the promises of God in those Scriptures. These Scriptures will help you keep your faith in God and to stand firm when you are under attack.

2 Chronicles 20:17 "You will not have to fight this battle. Take up your positions; stand firm and see the deliverance the Lord will give you, O Judah and Jerusalem. Do not be afraid; do not be discouraged. Go out to face them tomorrow, and the Lord will be with you."

Isaiah 7:9 "If you do not stand firm in your faith, you will not stand at all."

Isaiah 55:22 "Cast all your cares on the Lord and He will sustain you; He will never let the righteous fall."

Pray continually

This keeps you close to God and strengthened spiritually.

Luke 18:1 "Then Jesus told His disciples a parable to show them that they should always pray and not give up."

1 Thessalonians 5:16-18 "Be joyful always; pray continually; give thanks in all circumstances, for this is God's will for you in Christ Jesus."

Stay in the Word

It is your strength and your Amour. ONLY IN JESUS CAN YOU STAND AGAINST THE DEVIL'S ATTACKS AND WIN.

Philippians 4:13 "I can do everything through Him who gives me strength."

Psalm 1:2-3 "But his delight is in the law of the Lord, and on His law, he meditates day and night. He is like a tree planted by streams of water, which yields its fruit in season and whose leaf does not wither. Whatever he does prospers."

Psalm 18:30-32 "As for God, His way is perfect; the Word of the Lord is flawless. He is a shield for all who take refuge in Him. For who is God besides the Lord? And who is the Rock except our God? It is God who arms me with strength and makes my way perfect."

Psalm 19:7-9 "The law of the Lord is perfect, reviving the soul. The statutes of the Lord are trustworthy, making wise the simple. The precepts of the Lord are right, giving joy to the heart. The commands of the Lord are radiant, giving light to the eyes. The fear of the Lord is pure, enduring forever."

Psalm 33:4 "For the Word of the Lord is right and true; He is faithful in all He does."

(Psalm 119:105) "Your Word is a lamp to my feet and a light for my path."

John 6:35 "I am the bread of life. He who comes to me will never go hungry, and he who believes in me will never be thirsty."

John 6:47-48 "I tell you the truth; he who believes has everlasting life. I am the bread of life."

The Armor of the Lord

Ephesians 6:13-18

The belt of truth - Be truthful and sincere, and armed with the truth - which is the Word of God, deep within your mind and heart.

The breastplate of righteousness - the righteousness of Jesus, upon receiving Him into your heart is within you.

The gospel of peace - knowledge of the Word of God will help you to know His promises and will for you and how much He loves you. A love so great, it gives you eternal life. This will give you peace and help you to overcome evil attacks, so you can keep the peace. For He says, (Matthew 5:9) "Blessed are the peacemakers, for they will be called sons of God."

The shield of faith - Trust in God will always give you victory, peace, and the strength to endure.

The helmet of salvation - This is what you need first and foremost, without Jesus, as your Lord and Savior you will be fighting a losing battle. Knowing that you will spend an eternity in heaven where there will be peace and joy forever, with your Almighty Father, gives you great hope and arms you with the courage you need to go through your trials victoriously.

The sword of the Spirit - which is the Word of God. The Bible has an answer for every situation. The Bible gives you instructions on daily life and the promises of God. Reading and knowing the Word of God will help you fight off Satan and guard your mind. He will always try to distort the Word of God through false prophets and the thoughts he gives you. Knowing the Bible will help you keep Satan in his place.

Talking to God will keep you close to Him. A close relationship with God will help you to know that He loves you and will always be there for you. "Come near to God and He will come near to you" (James 4:8).

Fasting and Faith

This is one of the most forceful weapons. Fasting, along with prayer, lifts your spirits and strengthens your spirit because what your physical body is lacking in food, you are relying on the power and strength of God to keep you strong during your fasting and praying not only physically but spiritually as well.

Fasting is done in three ways: complete - without food or water; regular - without food only and drinking water, or partial - choosing to omit certain things. It can be done for any amount of time.

The fast that God chooses and lays on your heart is the one that is most effective and the one that will bring liberty as you follow it through to the end.

It must be sincere and totally faithful and fulfilled to the end. If God lays it on your heart to do, trust Him to supply all your needs to accomplish the task.

"And my God will meet all your needs according to His glorious riches in Christ Jesus" (Philippians 4:19).

Praise God for who He is, always. He is the Creator of the world. He is God. He is the Savior of your soul. For that alone He is worthy of praise!

2 Chronicles 20:21 "After consulting the people, Jehoshaphat appointed men to sing to the Lord and to praise Him for the splendor of His holiness as they went out at the head of the army, saying: 'Give thanks to the Lord, for His love endures forever."

Psalm 50:14-15 "Sacrifice thank offerings to God, fulfill your vows to the Most High, and call upon me in the day of trouble; I will deliver you, and you will honor me."

Psalm 50:23 "He who sacrifices thank offerings honors me, and He prepares the way so that I may show him the salvation of God."

As you do all these things stay confident in God - trusting He will deliver you.

Psalm 27:14 "Wait for the Lord; be strong and take heart and wait for the Lord."

Psalm 29:11 "The Lord gives strength to His people; the Lord blesses His people with peace."

Psalm 31:19 "How great is your goodness, which you have stored up for those who fear you, which you bestow in the sight of men on those who take refuge in you."

Psalm 33:11 "But the plans of the Lord stand firm forever, the purposes of His heart through all generations."

Psalm 34:17-19 "The righteous cry out, and the Lord hears them; He delivers them from all their troubles. The Lord is close to the brokenhearted and saves those who are crushed in spirit. A righteous man may have many troubles, but the Lord delivers him from them all."

Psalm 145:13 "The Lord is faithful to all His promises and loving toward all He has made."

Psalm 60:12 "With God we will gain the victory, and He will trample down our enemies."

John 15:7 "If you remain in me and My Words remain in you, ask whatever you wish, and it will be given you."

Standing Firm

Christians are not to run from trials like a coward. You have the Spirit of Jesus within you. You are making His Spirit run with you as you run. Jesus never backed down from the Pharisees. He did not back down from the cross. He carried it.

Luke 9:23 "If anyone would come after me, he must deny himself and take up his cross daily and follow me. For whoever wants to save his life will lose it, but whoever loses his life for me will save it."

We are to carry ours as well. When trouble comes, we are not to run in fear. This is not from God.

Romans 8:15 "For you did not receive a spirit that makes you a slave again to fear, but you received the Spirit of sonship. And by Him we cry, '*Abba*,' Father."

We are children of God! Royalty! Co-heirs with Christ! He was not a coward and we shouldn't be either. Living in fear is living in unbelief.

Romans 8:17-19 "Now if we are children, then we are heirs of God and co-heirs with Christ, if indeed we share in His sufferings in order that we may also share in His glory. I consider that our present sufferings are not worth comparing with the glory that will be revealed in us. The creation waits in eager expectation for the sons of God to be revealed."

When you run from problems, back down in fear, and get discouraged and depressed instead of standing firm and trusting God, you are doing the will of Satan and not God. If you want to obey and trust God, you must die to yourself and stand firm.

Isaiah 7:9 "If you do not stand firm in your faith, you will not stand at all."

God is the creator and He is more powerful than Satan and more powerful than our circumstances. Nothing is too hard for Him.

Jeremiah 32:27 "I am the Lord, the God of all mankind. Is anything too hard for Me?"

If you want to be delivered you must stand firm and trust God.

Hebrews 11:6 "And without faith it is impossible to please God, because anyone who comes to Him must believe that He exists and that He rewards those who earnestly seek Him."

Standing firm and trusting God will not only show God how devoted you are to Him, but it will also help you to grow and mature as a Christian. With each trial you overcome you get stronger through the loving guidance and strength of Jesus Christ.

Philippians 4:13 "I can do everything through Him who gives me strength."

You can then comfort and encourage others as God has comforted you.

2 Corinthians 1:3-4 "Praise be to the God and Father of our Lord Jesus Christ, the Father of compassion and the God of all comfort, who comforts us in all our troubles so that we can comfort those in any trouble with the comfort we ourselves have received from God."

How we go through trials and react to those around us who persecute us, to those who are evil and full of wickedness is a witness to them. What kind of witness do you want to be? The world expects us to react worldly, and Satan is always trying to lure us into a trap. He wants us to react to the evil and hatred that others, even our unsaved loved ones, overwhelm us with in a way the world would react; a way that is not becoming to a Christian. We are the light of the world from the Son of God who is within us.

Matthew 5:13-16 "You are the salt of the earth. But if the salt loses its saltiness, how can it be made salty again? It is no longer good for anything, except to be thrown out and trampled by men. You are the light of the world. A city on a hill cannot be hidden. Neither do people light a lamp and put it under a bowl. Instead, they put it on its stand, and it gives light to everyone in the house. In the same way, let your light shine before men, that they may see your good deeds and praise your Father in heaven."

We are to always clothe ourselves in the love of God and walk in Love in all we do.

Colossians 3:13-15 "Bear with each other and forgive whatever grievances you may have against one another. Forgive as the Lord forgave you. And over all these virtues put on love, which binds them all together in perfect unity. Let the peace of Christ rule in your hearts, since as members of one body you were called to peace. And be thankful."

II John 1:5-6 "I ask that we love one another. And this is love: that we walk in obedience to His commands. As you have heard from the beginning, His command is that you walk in love."

Deuteronomy 5:33 "Walk in all the way that the Lord your God has commanded you, so that you may live and prosper and prolong your days in the land that you will possess."

The world repays evil for evil. But God says to overcome it with love.

Romans 12:17-21 "Do not repay anyone evil for evil. Be careful to do what is right in the eyes of everybody. If it is possible, as far as it depends on you, live at peace with everyone. Do not take revenge, my friends, but leave room for God's wrath, for it is written: 'It is mine to avenge; I will repay, says the Lord. On the contrary: If your enemy is hungry, feed him; if he is thirsty, give him something to drink. In doing this, you will heap burning coals on his head. Do not be overcome by evil, but overcome evil with good."

That is what He did when He died on the cross. He overcame an evil world by His unselfish act of love when He took the sins of the world on His shoulders and died for us. He did this so we would receive forgiveness of our sins through His blood and by His love and have eternal life.

Romans 5:8 "But God demonstrates His own love for us in this: While we were still sinners, Christ died for us."

The way we act and react to unbelievers is a witness to them. It is a seed planted in their heart that God will cause to grow.

1 Corinthians 3:7-9 "So neither he who plants nor he who waters is anything, but only God, who makes things grow. The man who plants and the man who waters have one purpose, and each will be rewarded according to his own labor. For we are God's fellow workers; you are God's field, God's building."

This is an act of worship and service to God. He died for us. We are now called to be witnesses for Him in all we say and do and our facial and bodily expressions. Satan is always waiting and watching and is always ready to put the acts of Christians under a microscope to catch us doing something wrong.

1 Peter 5:8 "Be self-controlled and alert. Your enemy the devil prowls around like a roaring lion looking for someone to devour."

Be the witness that you were called to be. You were not saved to sit around on your easy chair and wait for the rapture to take place. Jesus carried His cross and witnessed to the world. We are to do the same. We already had our free ride. He took our punishment *for* us! Now it is time for us to do our part.

Matthew 28:19-20 "Therefore go and make disciples of all nations, baptizing them in the name of the Father and of the Son and of the Holy Spirit, and teaching them to obey everything I have commanded you. And surely, I am with you always, to the very end of the age."

In standing firm, you will be delivered, and God's purpose will prevail.

Isaiah 46:10 "I say: My purpose will stand, and I will do all that I please."

Proverbs 19:21 "Many are the plans in a man's heart, but it is the Lord's purpose that prevails."

Acts 16:24-26

Remember Paul and Silas when they were in Jail and singing hymns and songs to God? Their feet were fastened to the stocks. Our feet need to be fastened firm in our faith in God. As they were praising God, the other prisoners were listening and were set free as well as Paul and Silas. Seeing the faith of Paul and Silas in their midnight hour (overwhelming trial) affected the other prisoners, (the unsaved people you know).

Everyone's chains came loose! Praise God! Faith and witnessing in actions and speech have a rippling effect!

Stop Dancing With The Devil

Do you want victory in your life? Then stop inviting defeat! That is exactly what you are doing when you entertain, dwell on, and give in to every negative thought or emotion that comes into your mind! The battle is truly won or lost in your mind!

When you act on the negative thoughts or emotions or when you speak them you are inviting the devil into your life. The devil cannot read your thoughts. He can whisper negative thoughts into your mind, but he cannot read your mind. Only God can do that. When you speak that trash all you are doing is giving him more ammunition to use against you. Don't you have enough trials in your life? So, why are trying to create more? Stop that! God says, "We are more than conquerors." Act like it!

Victory is ours!

God promises us victory. He has already been through our trials ahead of us. He knows the path that you take. He knows the plans He has for you. He tells you what to do and how to overcome in His Word. Do not merely read it, do what it says.

Psalm 60:12 "With God we will gain the victory and He will trample down our enemies."

John 10:10 "The thief comes only to steal and kill and destroy; I have come that they may have life and have it to the full."

He tells us to take every thought captive.

2 Corinthians 10:4-5 "The weapons we fight with are not the weapons of the world. On the contrary, they have divine power to demolish strongholds. We demolish arguments and every pretension that sets itself up against the knowledge of God, and we take captive every thought to make it obedient to Christ."

That means if it does not agree with the word of God then trash it! Does God promise depression or joy? Does He promise victory or defeat? Does He promise reconciliation or separation? Does He promise poverty or blessings? Does He promise life everlasting or eternal death? As Joshua said, "Choose for yourselves this day whom you will serve, whether the gods your forefathers served beyond the River or the gods of the Amorites, in whose land you are living. But as for me and my household, we will serve the Lord." It means do not listen to negative speech or words spoken in hate. It is what God the Creator of Heaven and Earth and everything in it, the One who holds the power of life and death, it is what He says about you that counts. He says that you are the righteousness of God in Christ Jesus. He says that you were drawn with loving-kindness. He says that you are fearfully and wonderfully made!

Proverbs 15:4 "The tongue that brings healing is a tree of life."

Proverbs 16:17 "The highway of the upright avoids evil; he who guards his way guards his life."

Do you guard your way? Do you guard what your eyes and your ears take in? Do you guard what comes into your home? Or do you give in, in fear? "The fear of man will prove to be a snare." It shows you think that man has more power than God.

Psalm 118:6 "The Lord is with me; I will not be afraid. What can man do to me?"

Proverbs 16:24 "Pleasant words are a honeycomb, sweet to the soul and healing to the bones."

Proverbs 16:28 "A perverse man stirs up dissension, and a gossip separates close friends."

Power Is In Your Tongue

Proverbs 18:21 "The tongue has the power of life and death, and those who live it will eat its fruit."

What fruit do you want to partake in from what you say? Do you want blessings or more of the pain and frustrations that you are now experiencing? Have you wondered why you are not progressing in your spiritual walk or why the deep desires that God has planted in your heart have not come to pass? Get the tongue-o-meter out, the Bible, and examine your ways. Are speaking life over your circumstances or death?

Lamentations 3:40 "Let us examine our ways and test them and let us return to the Lord."
John 6:63 "The Spirit gives life; the flesh counts for nothing. The words I have spoken to you are spirit and they are life."

This means that whatever you speak is what you give life to. Everything takes time to grow, so if you are speaking life, give it time to grow. Every farmer plants seeds. He does not go out the very next day and expects a crop to harvest.

If you want a loved one to be saved speak it.

Acts 16:31 "Believe in the Lord Jesus, and you will be saved - you and your household."

Speak out, "My (husband, wife, child, brother, etc.) is saved!" Keep praying for this, and keep speaking and thanking God for it, and wait for it to happen! Expectation brings manifestation. If Jesus could conquer Satan in the desert by the Word of God, then we can too.

Psalm 22:3 "But thou art holy, O thou that inhabits the praises of Israel."

If God inhabits the praises of His people, then the opposite is true as well. When you speak negatively the pity parties you throw for yourself regularly give Satan glory. You permit him to invade more. Stop it! God says that we are victors, not victims.

As you stop speaking and dwelling on all that is negative, you must replace it. Not speaking it and trashing all the negativity is good, but unless you replace it with the positive, the negative will keep coming back. You must replace it with the promises of God concerning your situation.

Luke 11:23-26 "He who is not with me is against me, and he who does not gather with me, scatters. When an evil spirit comes out of a man, it goes through arid places seeking rest and does not find it. Then it says, 'I will return to the house I left.' When it arrives, it finds the house swept clean and put in order. Then it goes and takes seven other spirits more wicked than itself, and they go in and live there. And the final condition of that man is worse than the first."

Search the Bible and write His promises down and then stand on them. If it is good enough for God and our Lord and Savior, then it is good enough for us. He set the example that we should follow in His steps. He told us how to overcome and if we do not do what He says, then the lack of victory in our life is our fault, not His. If He told you that a certain person is holding $100,000.00 and it is yours. All you have to do is go and get it. If you do not go and get it, then don't complain about your financial hardship. He gave you the deliverance, but you did not receive it. Well, He gives us the deliverance and all we have to do is READ IT AND APPLY IT!

An idol, according to Webster's New American Dictionary, (1990, page 292) is anything that you give excessive devotion to. Dwelling on your problems continually and running after ways to deliver you instead of seeking *the way*, is seeking idols to deliver you instead of the deliverer. The Bible says to seek the kingdom first in order to seek God and His way of doing things. Are you seeking God for your financial troubles, or are you seeking money? If you are seeking money, then my dear beloved friend, you have made money your idol or your god whether you want to believe that or not. It is still the truth. Repent and change directions! Call out to the only one who saves and delivers. Seek Him, and He will take care of the rest.

Matthew 6:33 "But seek first the His kingdom and His righteousness, and all these things will be given to you as well."

Don't complain about your misery if you are not doing what the Bible says to do! From front to back, the Bible is God's love story about us and full of His promises and all we have to do is believe, confess, receive, and apply. The victory or lack of it is your choice. Our God is the only One who gives you a test with a multiple-choice question and the answer at the same time! How great is our God! Not only that, with God you will never fail! You get to take the test over and over until you pass it! The choice is yours. How many times do you want to take it?

Deuteronomy 30:19-20 "This day I call heaven and earth as witnesses against you that I have set before you life and death, blessings and curses. Now choose life, so that you and your children may live and that you may love the Lord your God, listen to His voice, and hold fast to Him. For the Lord is your life, and He will give you many years in the land He swore to give to your fathers, Abraham, Isaac, and Jacob."

Faith: The Power To What You Say & Believe

Romans 4:17 "God calls things that are not as though they were."

We must speak out about what we believe for. As you do that your faith will rise and that dark cloud in your heart will vanish. God is light and where there is light all darkness has to leave.

John 8:12 "I am the light of the world. Whoever follows me will never walk in darkness but will have the light of life."

Your faith is the electricity that connects to God's power. You believe and He acts.

Mark 11:24 "Therefore I tell you, whatever you ask for in prayer, believe that you have received it, and it will be yours."

Hebrews 11:1 "Now faith is being sure of what we hope for and certain of what we do not see."

Mark 9:23 "Everything is possible for him who believes."

The Lord says, "The righteous will live by faith. This pleases God. It tells Him you believe and trust Him to answer your prayers. Doesn't it bother you when people do not trust you, especially those that are close to you? Do you expect our Heavenly Father to be any different?

Hebrews 11:6 "And without faith it is impossible to please God, because anyone who comes to Him must believe that He exists that He rewards those who earnestly seek Him."

James 1:6-7 "But when he asks, he must believe and not doubt, because he who doubts is like a wave of the sea, blown and tossed by the wind. That man should not think he will receive anything from the Lord; he is a double-minded man, unstable in all he does."

If all you do is speak negative and doubt, that is what you will keep receiving. That is what the Word says. You will receive whatever you believe for. It does not have to stay that way.

Change directions!

Jeremiah 6:16 "Stand at the crossroads and look; ask for the ancient paths, ask where the good way is, and walk in it, and you will find rest for your souls."

Go on a fast, a fast of negative thinking and talking. Then speak out the positive in what God promises in His Word. Then watch the peace of God fill your heart and His promises start to come alive in your life.

Psalm 138:2 "For you have exalted above all things Your Name and Your Word."

Don't speak out every thought that comes into your mind. Judge it against the promises of God. If it does not agree, then dismiss it! But to do this there is a catch, **YOU MUST READ THE WORD TO KNOW IT.**

Genesis 1:3 "Let there be light." God spoke it and it came to be and if we were created in His image and He tells us in His Word that our words are spirit and life and we can do the same. We can frame our world with our words. He set the example. You must follow it to receive its reward.

If you have too much hell in your life, stop inviting it in! Dwell on and trust in God. He will give you peace and rest amid your trials. That is true victory. When Satan wants you to be down, depressed, and miserable and you are shouting, jumping for joy, and praising God instead. Do you want true victory? Start now!

Isaiah 26:3-4 "You will keep in perfect peace him whose mind is steadfast because he trusts in you. Trust in the Lord forever, for the Lord, the Lord, is the Rock eternal."

The Battle Belongs To The Lord

We are small; our problems are big, but God is Bigger!

Know who the battle belongs to!

John 4:4 "You, dear children, are from God and have overcome them, because the One who is in you is greater than the one who is in the world."

The Word of God says, "In this world, you will have trouble. But take heart! I have overcome the world," (John 16:33). We are going to go through trials of all kinds. We have big problems, but we also have a *big God!* Jesus went through His time of testing and overcame and with His Spirit within us, we can overcome as well. Just believe God. Believe His Word and the promises it has for our lives. Part of overcoming is realizing who the battle really belongs to. It belongs to God. Ever since Satan was cast from heaven, he has been determined to destroy the things of God. He has been at war with God.

John 10:10 "The thief comes only to steal and kill and destroy; I have come that they may have life and have it to the full."

1 Samuel 17:47 "All those gathered here will know that it is not by sword or spear that the Lord saves; for the battle is the Lord's, and He will give all of you into our hands."

2 Chronicles 20:15 "Do not be afraid or discouraged because of this vast army; for the battle is not yours, but God's."

The Israelites were faced with a battle against the Philistines. Goliath, one of the Philistines who was about 9 feet tall, came forward with a proposition of just him against one of the Israelites.

1 Samuel 17:4 "A champion named Goliath, who was from Gath, came out of the Philistine camp. He was over nine feet tall."

Goliath represents how Satan, who is bigger and stronger than we are and so are the trials that come our way. You cannot fight Satan and win. He is out of your league, but he is not out of God's. God created him. God is stronger. The created is *not* more powerful than the creator. "A student is not above his teacher, nor a servant above his master" (Matthew 10:24).

Stop fighting him. Give the battle back to God where it belongs! Let God be God and do His job!

Ephesians 6:12 "For our struggle is not against flesh and blood, but against the rulers, against the authorities, against the powers of this dark world and against the spiritual forces of evil in the heavenly realms."

Is your problem as big as the one the Israelites faced? David was only a boy and Goliath was a man experienced in fighting and 9 feet tall! We face problems that big and are defeated every time we worry over them instead of giving them over to God. The only way to victory is to let God do the fighting! Does your problem instill fear in you as it did to the Israelites? "On hearing the Philistine's words, Saul and all the Israelites were dismayed and terrified," (1 Samuel 17:11). Satan instills fear. Fear is not from God.

Romans 8:15 "For you did not receive a spirit that makes you a slave again to fear, but you received the Spirit of sonship. And by Him we cry, '*Abba*,' Father."

In God's hands, the problem is smaller than it looks!

Satan will make you look at the giant size problem that you are facing and cause you to take your eyes off Jesus. This keeps the problem in your hands instead of God's where it belongs. Satan does this to instill fear in you and make you give up and turn away from Jesus. You start to worry about how you are going to get through it, which takes your peace and joy away. Do not give in to this! Resist the devil and his schemes!

Isaiah 26:3 "You will keep in perfect peace him whose mind is steadfast, because he trusts in you."

2 Corinthians 4:18 "So we fix our eyes not on what is seen, but on what is unseen. For what is seen is temporary, but what is unseen is eternal."

James 4:7-8 "Submit yourselves, then, to God. Resist the devil, and he will flee from you. Come near to God and He will come near to you."

As you give the problem completely over to God and trust Him to take care of it, your peace and joy return. Ask Jesus to help you to keep your eyes on Him. Ask Him to reveal Scriptures to you as you read the Bible that will help you trust Him to give you victory in your trials. The victory is already yours; you just have to believe and receive it. Receive it by trusting God that your bills are paid then He will provide the means for you to pay them. Trust Him that your lost loved ones are saved, and He will direct their steps.

Proverbs 3:5-6 "Trust in the Lord with all your heart and lean not on your own understanding; in all your ways acknowledge Him, and He will make your paths straight."

Proverbs 20:24 "A man's steps are directed by the Lord. How then can anyone understand his own way."

Jeremiah 29:11-14 " For I know the plans I have for you, declares the Lord, plans to prosper you and not to harm you, plans to give you hope and a future. Then you will call upon Me and come and pray to Me, and I will listen to you. You will seek Me and find Me when you seek Me with all your heart. I will be found by you, declares the Lord, and bring you back from captivity."

Hebrews 12:1-2 "Therefore, since we are surrounded by such a great cloud of witnesses, let us throw off everything that hinders and the sin that so easily entangles, and let us run with perseverance the race marked out for us. Let us fix our eyes on Jesus, the author and perfecter of our faith, who for the joy set before Him endured the cross, scorning its shame, and sat down at the right hand of the throne of God."

Philippians 4:19 "And my God will meet all your needs according to His glorious riches in Christ Jesus."

John 14:26 "But the Counselor, the Holy Spirit, whom the Father will send in My name, will teach you all things and will remind you of everything I have said to you."

Acts 16:31 "Believe in the Lord Jesus, and you will be saved - you and your household."

With Jesus, though you are small, just like David and your problem is big, just like Goliath, you will be victorious. The Lord will give you courage and strength just as He did for David. Part of being victorious is being able to praise God for the victory that you know is yours before you receive it. Amid your trial, before the money or job comes to help you pay your bills, or before your lost loved one is saved, you can praise God because you know and are sure of the coming deliverance and an-swered prayers! That is true victory! Victory, that while Satan is trying to discourage and depress you, you are praising God instead! Don't you know that really irritates Satan?

Psalm 50:14-15 "Sacrifice thank offerings to God, fulfill your vows to the Most High, and call upon me in the day of trouble; I will deliver you, and you will honor Me."

Philippians 4:6 "Do not be anxious about anything, but in everything, by prayer and petition with thanksgiving, present your requests to God."

Hebrews 11:1 "Faith is being sure of what we hope for and certain of what we do not see."

1 Samuel 17:32 "Let no one lose heart on account of this Philistine; your servant will go and fight him."

1 Samuel 17:37 "The Lord who delivered me from the paw of the lion and the paw of the bear will deliver me from the hand of the Philistine."

Jesus is bigger and stronger than our enemy, the devil, and any trial that he will throw our way. All we have to do to receive the victory that He promises us is to just believe Him and accept that our answered prayers are on the way.

1 Samuel 17:45 "David said to the Philistine, 'You come against me with sword and spear and javelin, but I come against you in the name of the Lord Almighty, the God of the armies of Israel, whom you have defied."

1 Corinthians 1:25 "For the foolishness of God is wiser than man's wisdom, and the weakness of God is stronger than man's strength."

David knew that the Lord would bring victory and he didn't look at the size of Goliath, but rather the size and power of God. We serve a mighty God. He is bigger than any problem that may come against us and the end is always the same, we win!

Psalm 24:8 "Who is this King of glory? The Lord strong and mighty, the Lord mighty in battle."

Psalm 60:12 "With God we will gain the victory, and He will trample down our enemies."

Psalm 147:5 "Great is our Lord and mighty in power; His understanding has no limit."

1 Corinthians 15:57-58 "He gives us the victory through our Lord Jesus Christ. Therefore, my dear brothers, stand firm. Let nothing move you. Always give yourselves fully to the work of the Lord, because you know that your labor in the Lord is not in vain."

Operate in faith and knowledge of your coming victory!

Great faith and perseverance in God will move God to give you the victory. Do not fear or doubt. Satan will throw many things your way. Your lost loved one will get worse, or more bills will come up, and the job you are interviewing for goes to someone else. Jesus says to not be afraid. This is a sure sign that victory is around the corner. When victory for you is near, Satan will throw more bad things your way to make you give up. God is a God of love and the bad things that come your way are not from Him. They are from Satan and the consequences of what you have sown in your life. So, now that you know his tactics, as you see more bad things coming, praise God! For your victory is near!

James 1:16-17 "Don't be deceived, my dear brothers. Every good and perfect gift is from above, coming down from the Father of heavenly lights, who does not change like the shifting shadows."

Matthew 15:28 "Woman, you have great faith! Your request is granted."

Matthew 17:20 "Because you have so little faith. I tell you the truth, if you have faith as small as a mustard seed, you can say to this mountain, 'Move from here to there' and it will move. Nothing will be impossible for you."

Hebrews 10:22-23 "Let us draw near to God with a sincere heart in full assurance of faith, having our hearts sprinkled to cleanse us from a guilty conscience and having our bodies washed with pure water. Let us hold unswervingly to the hope we profess, for He who promised is faithful."

Hebrews 10:35-38 "So do not throw away your confidence; it will be richly rewarded. You need to persevere so that when you have done the will of God, you will receive what He has promised. For in just a very little while, 'He who is coming will come and will not delay. But my righteous one will live by faith. And if he shrinks back, I will not be pleased with him.'"

1 Corinthians 16:13-14 "Be on your guard; stand firm in the faith; be men of courage; be strong. Do everything in love."

Do not fear or doubt. This tells God that you do not trust Him or believe in His power to save and deliver you. This does not please Him and will not bring about your deliverance.

Hebrews 11:6 "And without faith it is impossible to please God, because anyone who comes to Him must believe that He exists and that He rewards those who earnestly seek Him."

Ask God to deliver you from the fears that you have. He will deliver you from them, helping you to trust Him to give you the victory you are praying for. Giving the problems over to God and letting Him fight the battle, gives Him the glory. It will be God's hand giving you the victory just as He did for David.

Psalm 34:4 "I sought the Lord, and He answered me; He delivered me from all my fears."

Zechariah 4:6 "Not by might nor by power, but by My Spirit,' says the Lord Almighty."

Trust in God; He will save you and deliver you from all your troubles and heal all of your wounds whether they are physical, emotional, spiritual, or financial.

Psalm 34:17-20 "The righteous cry out, and the Lord hears them; He delivers them from all their troubles. The Lord is close to the brokenhearted and saves those who are crushed in spirit. A righteous man may have many troubles, but the Lord delivers him from them all; He protects all his bones, not one of them will be broken."

Jeremiah 30:17 "But I will restore you to health and heal all your wounds,' declares the Lord."

God, who is the Creator of heaven and earth, the One who gives life and saves us, the One who created everything in the heavens and the earth, has the power to deliver and save you from anything.

Jeremiah 32:26 "I am the Lord, the God of all mankind. Is anything too hard for me?"

Isaiah 43:13 "No one can deliver out of my hand. When I act, who can reverse it?"

Isaiah 35:4 "Be strong, do not fear; your God will come, He will come with vengeance; with divine retribution He will come to save you."

As small as David was, he knew and trusted in the power of God and dared anyone to defy God.

1 Samuel 17:26 "Who is this uncircumcised Philistine that he should defy the armies of the living God?"

1 Samuel 17:32 "Let no one lose heart on account of this Philistine; your servant will go and fight him."

Our victory is already declared in Jesus Christ!

God gave him the victory. David, being small, and Goliath so big, left no doubt that it was God who gave them the victory. God was glorified that day. This is what God wants in all of our lives. When God is glorified the lives of other people are touched by it and are saved.

1 Samuel 17:50 "So David triumphed over the Philistine with a sling and a stone; without a sword in his hand, he struck down the Philistine and killed him."

Isaiah 42:8 "I am the Lord; that is my name! I will not give my glory to another or my praise to idols."

Isaiah 45:5 "I am the Lord, and there is no other; apart from me there is no God."

Isaiah 43:6-7 "Bring My sons and daughters from the ends of the earth - everyone who is called by my name, whom I created for my glory, whom I formed and made."

1 Corinthians 1:27-31 "But God chose the foolish things of the world to shame the wise; God chose the weak things of the world to shame the strong. He chose the lowly things of this world and the despised things - and the things that are not - to nullify the things that are, so that no one may boast before Him. It is because of Him that you are in Christ Jesus, who God - that is, our righteousness, holiness, and redemption. Therefore, as it is written: 'Let him who boasts boast in the Lord.'"

Have faith in God and who He is. Have faith in His Sovereign power. Have faith in His authority. Have faith in His love, mercy, and forgiveness. Though you are small, and your problem is big; God is great, and He is bigger. Let Him be glorified in you and your life. Give everything over to God from your smallest problem to your biggest. You will prevail and your victory will come!

Isaiah 66:5-6 "Hear the word of the Lord, you who tremble at His word: 'Your brothers who hate you, and exclude you because of my name, have said, 'Let the Lord be glorified, that we may see your joy!' Yet they will be put to shame. Hear the uproar from the city; hear that noise from the temple! It is the sound of the Lord repaying His enemies all they deserve."

Romans 8:17-18 "Now if we are children, then we are heirs of God and co-heirs with Christ, if indeed we share in His sufferings in order that we may share in His glory. I consider that our present sufferings are not worth comparing with the glory that will be revealed in us."

2 Thessalonians 1:11-12 "We constantly pray for you, that our God may count you worthy of His calling, and that by His power He may fulfill every good purpose of yours and every act prompted by your faith. We pray this so that the name of our Lord Jesus may be glorified in you and you in Him, according to the grace of our God and the Lord Jesus Christ."

In trusting God and letting go of your problems, truly giving them over to God, and submitting to God, your worry leaves, and your peace returns. It is just like handing a bill over to someone else to pay. It sure feels good to give it away! This is how we must treat every problem we have and when we do, we will feel that same relief and that same peace of mind and heart. When you do this, you come through victoriously. You come through "as gold." Only in Jesus Christ is your guaranteed victory; victory over sin and victory passing through our trials, and in our answered prayers.

Job 22:21 "Submit to God and be at peace with Him; in this way, prosperity will come to you."

Job 23:10 "But He knows the way that I take; when He has tested me, I will come forth as gold."

Job 42:2 "I know that you can do all things; no plan of yours can be thwarted."

Psalm 44:6-8 "I do not trust in my bow, my sword does not bring me victory; but you give us victory over our enemies, you put our adversaries to shame. In God, we make our boast all day long, and we will praise your name forever."

1 Corinthians 15:54-58 "Death has been swallowed up in victory. Where, O death, is your victory? Where, O death, is your sting? The sting of death is sin, and the power of sin is the law. But thanks be to God! He gives us the victory through our Lord Jesus Christ. Therefore, my dear brothers, stand firm. Let nothing move you. Always give yourselves fully to the work of the Lord, because you know that your labor in the Lord is not in vain."

CHAPTER 5

Blessed By God

This is a chapter that everyone wants to read; studies on how to be blessed by God! But the true blessings of God come automatically when we put Him first and seek to do His will. When we put Him and His purpose and His people first as He did for us when He died for us; then He will take care of us and all of our needs and deepest desires.

(Matthew 6:33) "Seek first His kingdom and His righteousness and all these things will be given to you as well."

Selfishness does not have a place in the kingdom of God. (James 3:16) "For where you have envy and selfish ambition, there you find disorder and every evil practice." The death and resurrection of our Lord and Savior Jesus Christ is an explanation in itself of the love of God. His unselfish act of love shows us how we are to live. (John 15:12-13) "My command is this: Love each other as I have loved you. Greater love has no one than this that he lay down his life for his friends."

God wants to bless you and shower you with good gifts; just as any parent does; He just does not want the gifts to have you. When the material possessions of the world have you, then they take the place of God and become an idol to you. We are to have only one god and that is God Almighty. Seek after Him, learn His ways and He will shower you with blessings, He came to give us "life more abundantly."

Learn through studying the Bible and the studies in this book how to walk with God and grow closer to Him. Learn how to obey Him, worship Him, and serve Him and His people. Learn what it means to tithe. Tithing will bless you in more ways than just getting your money back. It teaches you to give; in giving you are not just giving to the church you belong to; you are indeed giving to God and in all that you give you become a part of everything done for the people your church helps.

(1 Timothy 6:17-19) "Command those who are rich in this present world not to be arrogant nor to put their hope in wealth, which is so uncertain, but to put their hope in God, who richly provides us with everything for our enjoyment. Command them to do good, to be rich in good deeds, and to be generous and willing to share. In this way, they will lay up treasure for themselves as a firm foundation for the coming age, so that they may take hold of the life that is truly life."

You may not always be there in person, but you will be in spirit through your giving and God will bless you in return.

(Psalm 31:19) "How great is your goodness, which you have stored up for those who fear you, which you bestow in the sight of men on those who take refuge in you."

I Am In My Father's House

Luke 15:11-12 "There was a man who had two sons. The younger one said to his father, 'Father, give me my share of the estate.' So, he divided his property between them."

Luke 15:28-32 "The older brother became angry and refused to go in. So, his father went out and pleaded with him. But he answered his father, 'Look! All these years I've been slaving for you and never disobeyed your orders. Yet you never gave me even a young goat, so I could celebrate with my friends. But when this son of yours who has squandered your property with prostitutes comes home, you kill the fattened calf for him!' 'My son,' the father said, 'you are always with me, and everything I have is yours. But we had to celebrate and be glad because this brother of yours was dead and is alive again; he was lost and is found.'"

Troubles surrounding you? Maybe you have taken your eyes off Jesus!

Are you surrounded by troubles? Bills are bombarding you from every direction and one thing after another popping up without warning to extract even more of the money that you do not have enough to go around. You are wondering, where is it going to come from? Maybe it isn't money that's the problem. Maybe it is a relationship gone badly or children headed down the wrong path. Maybe it is all of the above.

If you are a child of God then as the son that stayed behind and was obedient, everything that the father had was his. So, it is with us. You have taken your eyes off of Jesus. Remember Peter? He had the faith to walk on water as long as he kept his eyes on Jesus. When he took his eyes off Him and started looking at his circumstances, fear set in. Fear is not from God!! It is of the devil! Don't give in to it! Walk on afraid and overcome!

Matthew 14:29-30 "Then Peter got down out of the boat, walked on the water and came toward Jesus. But when he saw the wind, he was afraid and, beginning to sink, cried out, 'Lord, save me!"

Hebrews 12:1-3 "Therefore, since we are surrounded by such a great cloud of witnesses, let us throw off everything that hinders and the sin that so easily entangles, and let us run with perseverance the race marked out for us. Let us fix our eyes on Jesus, the author and perfecter of our faith, who for the joy set before Him endured the cross, scorning its shame, and sat down at the right hand of the throne of God. Consider Him who endured such opposition from sinful men, so that you will not grow weary and lose heart."

Romans 8:15-17 "For you did not receive a spirit of fear, but you received the Spirit of sonship. And by Him, we cry, 'Abba, Father.' The Spirit Himself testifies with our spirit that we are God's children. Now if we are children, then we are heirs of God and co-heirs with Christ, if indeed we share in His sufferings in order that we may also share in His glory."

Trials are to mold you, weed out the bad, and strengthen the good. Learn from them. Don't run!

Satan wants to destroy our testimony. He wants to steal your joy and your victory. Get some spiritual backbone! Walk on! Do it afraid! Dare to keep believing, to keep trusting, if not for your promised victory, and do it just to spite Satan!

Hebrews 11:6 "And without faith it is impossible to please God, because anyone who comes to Him must believe that He exists and that He rewards those who earnestly seek Him."

John 10:10 "The thief comes to steal and kill and destroy; I have come that they may have life, and have it to the full."

Psalm 145:13 "The Lord is faithful to all His promises and loving toward all He has made."

Psalm 60:12 "With God we will gain the victory, and He will trample down our enemies."

Satan isn't going to just sit back and make it easy for you. He didn't make it easy for Jesus, the Son of God! He will not make it easy for you either. Everyone in life will go through troubles and hardships, but as a child of God, your outcome will always be one of victory if you persevere; not only that, but you also have eternal life, not so with those who choose to reject Jesus and follow their own way and the ways of the world.

John 2:15-17 "Do not love the world or anything in the world. If anyone loves the world, the love of the Father is not in him. For everything in the world - the cravings of sinful man, the lust of his eyes, and the boasting of what he has and does - comes not from the Father but from the world. The world and its desires pass away, but the man who does the will of God lives forever."

Proverbs 18:10 "The name of the Lord is a strong tower; the righteous run to it and are safe."

James 5:11 "As you know, we consider blessed those who have persevered. You have heard of Job's perseverance and have seen what the Lord finally brought about. The Lord is full of compassion and mercy."

You will go through many trials. They are to help you grow and mature as a child of God. You have years of the world in you and when you first receive Jesus you are not automatically the perfect Christian. The trials you go through will increase your faith and clean out all the impurities in your heart, which in turn will help the fruit of the Spirit, grow within you. At conversion, God gives you a new spirit, the Spirit of Jesus Christ. Trials will help that Spirit to grow and weed out everything impure and unholy.

James 1:2-5 "Consider it pure joy, my brothers, whenever you face trials of many kinds because you know that the testing of your faith develops perseverance. Perseverance must finish its work so that you may be mature and complete, not lacking anything. If any of you lacks wisdom, he should ask God, who gives generously to all without finding fault, and it will be given to him."

1 Peter 1:6-7 "In this you greatly rejoice, though now for a little while you may have had to suffer grief in all kinds of trials. These have come so that your faith—of greater worth than gold, which perishes even though refined by fire - may be proven genuine and may result in praise, glory, and honor when Jesus Christ is revealed."

1 Thessalonians 5:23 "May God Himself, the God of peace, sanctify you through and through."

Matthew 15:13 "Every plant that My heavenly Father has not planted will be pulled up by the roots."

Jeremiah 18:6 "O house of Israel, can I not do with you as this potter does?" declares the Lord. "Like clay in the hands of the potter, so are you in My hand, O house of Israel."

Romans 8:28 "And we know that in all things God works for the good of those who love Him, who have been called according to His purpose."

Ezekiel 36:26 "I will give you a new heart and put a new spirit in you; I will remove from you your heart of stone and give you a heart of flesh."

Galatians 4:6-7 "Because you are sons, God sent the Spirit of His Son into our hearts, the Spirit who calls out, "*Abba*, Father.' So, you are no longer a slave, but a son; and since you are a son, God has made you also an heir."

Galatians 3:14 "He redeemed us in order that the blessing given to Abraham might come to the Gentiles through Christ Jesus, so that by faith we might receive the promise of the Spirit."

Galatians 5:22-23 "But the fruit of the Spirit is love, joy, peace, patience, kindness, goodness, faithfulness, gentleness and self-control."

The Lord is faithful to His Promises. Keep believing!

The Lord is not without compassion. He knows that trials are difficult, heartbreaking, and hard to bear. That is why He gave us His Spirit. As you renew your mind and your heart by staying close to God, your spirit-led ways become stronger. This helps you to say "no" to the carnal nature and the ways of the world and helps you to hold on to the promise that God gave you. He is faithful to His promises and will lead you to victory.

Lamentations 3:22-23 "Because of the Lord's great love we are not consumed, for His compassion never fails. They are new every morning; great is your faithfulness."

Psalm 117:1-2 "Praise the Lord, all you nations; extol Him, all you peoples. For great is His love toward us, and the faithfulness of the Lord endures forever."

Deuteronomy 31:6 "He will never leave you nor forsake you."

Matthew 11:28-30 "Come to me, all you who are weary and burdened, and I will give you rest. Take my yoke upon you and learn from me, for I am gentle and humble in heart, and you will find rest for your souls. For My yoke is easy and my burden is light."

John 4:16-18 "And so we know and rely on the love God has for us. God is love. Whoever lives in love lives in God, and God in Him. In this way, love is made complete among us so that we will have confidence on the day of judgment because in this world we are like Him. There is no fear in love. But perfect love drives out fear because fear has to do with punishment. The one who fears is not made perfect in love."

Romans 12:2 "Do not conform any longer to the pattern of this world but be transformed by the renewing of your mind."

Galatians 5:16 "So I say, live by the Spirit, and you will not gratify the desires of the sinful nature."

Titus 2:11-14 "For the grace of God that brings salvation has appeared to all men. It teaches us to say 'No' to ungodliness and worldly passions, and to live self-controlled, upright, and godly lives in this present age, while we wait for the blessed hope - the glorious appearing of our great God and Savior, Jesus Christ, who gave Himself for us to redeem us from all wickedness and to purify for Himself a people that are His very own, eager to do what is good."

No matter what you are going through, remember that you are a child of God and just as Jesus did not let Peter fall when he took his eyes off of Him, He will not let you fall either. When you get overwhelmed by your circumstances, remember God is always there for you. He held out His hand for Peter and He is holding His hand out for you as well. He loved you enough to die for you. He wants only your best.

Matthew 14:31 "Immediately Jesus reached out His hand and caught him."

Psalm 145:14 "The Lord upholds all those who fall and lifts up all who are bowed down."

Psalm 34:17-19 "The righteous cry out, and the Lord hears them; He delivers them from all their troubles. The Lord is close to the brokenhearted and saves those who are crushed in spirit. A righteous man may have many troubles, but the Lord delivers him from them all."

Jeremiah 29:11-14 "For I know the plans I have for you, declares the Lord, plans to prosper you and not to harm you, plans to give you hope and a future. Then you will call upon Me and come and pray to Me, and I will listen to you. You will seek Me and find Me when you seek Me with all your heart. I will be found by you, declares the Lord, and bring you back from captivity."

John 16:33 "I have told you these things, so that in me you may have peace. In this world, you will have trouble. But take heart! I have overcome the world."

In Christ, you have all that you need! Just ask for it, wait for it, and believe until you receive it!

Ephesians 1:3 "Praise be to the God and Father of our Lord Jesus Christ, who has blessed us in the heavenly realms with every spiritual blessing in Christ."

When you were a child at home your parents provided for you. They provided a roof over your head, and food to eat. They paid the water and electric bills and provided you with clothes. God is your heavenly Father. He will provide those same things, as you trust in Him. "My son," the father said, 'you are always with me, and everything I have is yours. But we had to celebrate and be glad because this brother of yours was dead and is alive again; he was lost and is found." (Luke 15:31-32)

Matthew 6:33 "But seek first His kingdom and His righteousness, and all these things will be given to you as well."

Psalm 24:1 "The earth is the Lord's, and everything in it, the world, and all who live in it; for He founded it upon the seas and established it upon the waters."

Jeremiah 27:5 "With My great power and outstretched arm I made the earth and its people and the animals that are on it, and I give it to anyone I please."

All you have to do is call upon the Lord and then trust Him to answer your prayer, but you must give Him time. You can't just snap your fingers at God and expect Him to jump to it. Remember He is God, and you are not. Trust Him to answer but in the time and way that is best for you. Remember how you are with your own child. You always want to bless them. Sometimes the things that they want, or you want to give them take longer than they want to wait. So, it is with our answered prayers. Keep trusting, tithing, obeying, and walking in God's love and your prayers will be answered.

Ecclesiastes 8:6 "For there is a proper time and procedure for every matter, though a man's misery weighs heavily upon him."

Ecclesiastes 3:1 "There is a time for everything and a season for every activity under heaven."

Mark 11:24 "Therefore I tell you, whatever you ask for in prayer, believe that you have received it, and it will be yours."

Psalm 23:1-4 "The Lord is my Shepherd, I shall not be in want. He makes me lie down in green pastures, He leads me beside quiet waters, and He restores my soul. He guides me in paths of righteousness for His name's sake."

Deuteronomy 11:22-23 "If you carefully observe all these commands, I am giving you to follow - to love the Lord your God, to walk in all His ways and to hold fast to Him - then the Lord will drive out all these nations before you, and you will dispossess nations larger and stronger than you."

You must have patience with God. After all, He has had patience with you in coming to Him. So, you must be patient with Him. Persistence, trust, and waiting on God will bring forth your deliverance. He doesn't always answer when you cry out to Him the first time. Don't give up. Keep trying.

2 Peter 3:19 "He is patient with you, not wanting anyone to perish, but everyone to come to repentance."

Psalm 27:14 "Wait for the Lord; be strong and take heart and wait for the Lord."

Luke 18:1 "Then Jesus told His disciples a parable to show them that they should always pray and not give up."

James 4:2 "You do not have, because you do not ask God."

You are God's child. Trust Him to provide for you. He is Jehovah Jireh! El Shaddai! He is your Father and He will provide! YOU ARE IN YOUR FATHER'S HOUSE!

Luke 21:19 "By standing firm you will gain life."

By standing firm you will gain life, resurrecting life for everything you are praying for, for everything dead in your life that needs to be raised to everlasting life. No matter what it is, a health problem that you need healing for, a lost loved one or friend that needs salvation, financial trouble and not enough money to go around, emotional issues, or a relationship gone bad that needs saved. Whatever it is that you are praying for, keep praying. Don't give up! You will gain life if you stand firm and God's blessings will chase you down! God is God all by Himself and is "able to do immeasurably more than all we ask or imagine," but He doesn't want to be just a *911* God. He wants to be your God, your Heavenly Father, your Savior, and your Friend of Friends and Everlasting Prince of Peace. Not just a God that you call on when you are in trouble, or you need something. This is why some of our prayers may take a little while, and the prayers involving someone else's will need to be worked out. Faith is believing without seeing, or it wouldn't be faith. We are to keep our eyes on Jesus and not on the circumstances of our trial. God is faithful and will answer your prayers!

2 Corinthians 5:7 "We live by faith, not by sight."

2 Corinthians 4:18 "So we fix our eyes not on what is seen, but on what is unseen. For what is seen is temporary, but what is unseen is eternal."

Psalm 147:14 "He grants peace to your borders and satisfies you with the finest of wheat."

Psalm 145:15-20 "The eyes of all look to you, and you give them their food at the proper time. You open your hand and satisfy the desires of every living thing. The Lord is righteous in all His ways and loving toward all He has made. The Lord is near to all who call on Him, to all who call on Him in truth. He fulfills the desires of those who fear Him; He hears their cry and saves them. The Lord watches over all who love Him, but all the wicked He will destroy."

Keeping The Sabbath Day Holy

Going to Church

Exodus 20:3-4 "You shall have no other gods before me. You shall not make for yourself an idol." *(Anything you put before worshiping God is your idol: work, drinking, drugs, yourself, etc.)*

Exodus 16:29 "Bear in mind that the Lord has given you the Sabbath; that is why on the sixth day He gives you bread for two days. Everyone is to stay where he is on the seventh day; no one is to go out."

Exodus 20:8 "Remember the Sabbath day by keeping it holy. Six days you shall work, but the seventh day is a Sabbath to the Lord your God."

Matthew 4:10 "Worship the Lord your God and serve Him only."

We are called to worship God; worship that is based on our love and devotion to Him from a grateful heart that is full of gratitude for Him for who He is and the eternal salvation that He has given us. Worship must be sincere. In true worship, the focus is totally on God and not on us or how we look to everyone else. True worship is all the time. God is your God all the time, not just in the good times.

Hebrews 10:22 "Let us draw near to God with a sincere heart in full assurance of faith."

John 4:23 "God is Spirit, and His worshipers must worship in spirit and in truth."

Psalm 33:1-3 "Sing to the Lord, you are righteous; it is fitting for the upright to praise Him. Praise the Lord with the harp; make music to Him on the ten-stringed lyre. Sing to Him a new song; play skillfully, and shout for joy."

Psalm 100:2 "Worship the Lord with gladness; come before Him with joyful songs.

Psalm 103:21-22 "So the name of the Lord will be declared in Zion and His praise in Jerusalem when the peoples and the kingdoms assemble to worship the Lord."

Psalm 134:2 "Lift up your hands in the sanctuary and praise the Lord."

Psalm 147:7 "Sing to the Lord with thanksgiving; make music to our God on the harp."

Psalm 149:1 "Praise the Lord, sing to the Lord a new song, His praise in the assembly of the saints."

Psalm 149:3 "Let them praise His name with dancing and make music to Him with tambourine and harp."

Acts 20:7 "On the first day of the week we came together to break bread." *(The disciples changed the Sabbath to Sunday in remembrance of the resurrection of Jesus Christ.)*

Call to Church

Matthew 16:18 "And I tell you that you are Peter, and on this rock, I will build my church, and the gates of Hades will not overcome it." -

This is talking about Peter's faith, not him and the church is us-the body of believers.

1 Corinthians 12:12-14 "The body is a unit, though it is made up of many parts; and though all its parts are many, they form one body. So, it is with Christ. For we were all baptized by one Spirit into one body - whether Jews or Greeks, slave or free - and we were all given the one Spirit to drink. Now the body is not made up of one part but of many."

Deuteronomy 4:10 "Remember the day you stood before the Lord your God at Horeb, when He said to me, 'Assemble the people before Me to hear My Words so that they may learn to revere Me as long as they live in the land and may teach them to their children.'"

We are called to go to church and to be a part of God's church out of our devotion to Him. We are encouraged by other believers; we learn from the Scriptures and sermons the Pastor is teaching and are strengthened by God's Word. You do not go because everyone else is doing it, or because you think if you go you won't go to hell. The only way to eternal life is through Jesus Christ. "Salvation is found in no one else, for there is no other name under heaven given to men by which we must be saved," (Acts 4:12). "That if you confess with your mouth, 'Jesus is Lord,' and believe in your heart that God raised Him from the dead, you will be saved. For it is with your heart that you believe and are justified, and it is with your mouth that you confess and are saved," (Romans 10:9-10).

1 Corinthians 12:12-13 "The body is a unit, though it is made up of many parts; and though all its parts are many, they form one body. So it is with Christ. For we were all baptized by one Spirit into one body - whether Jews or Greeks, slave or free - and we were all given the one Spirit to drink."

1 Corinthians 12:24-26 "But God has combined the members of the body and has given greater honor to the parts that lacked it, so that there should be no division in the body, but that its parts should have equal concern for each other. If one part suffers, every part suffers with it; if one part is honored, every part rejoices with it."

1 Timothy 4:13 "Until I come, devote yourself to the public reading of Scripture, to preaching and teaching."

Hebrews 10:25 "Let us not give up meeting together, as some are in the habit of doing."

Ephesians 5:23 "Christ is the head of the Church."

Colossians 1:17-18 "He is before all things, and in Him all things hold together. And He is the head of the body, the church; He is the beginning and the firstborn from among the dead, so that in everything He might have the supremacy."

Acts 20:28 "Keep watch over yourselves and all the flock which the Holy Spirit has made you overseers. Be shepherds of the church of God, which he bought with His own blood."

Tithe

Tithing is an act of worship that we are all called to do. God wants to be first in our life since He sent His One and Only Son to suffer and die for our sins out of His enormous love for us; He put us first and He wants to be first in our finances as well.

Exodus 23:19 "Bring the best of the first fruits of your soil to the house of the Lord your God."

Leviticus 24:8-9 "This bread is to be set out before the Lord regularly, Sabbath after Sabbath, on behalf of the Israelites, as a lasting covenant. It belongs to Aaron and his sons, who are to eat it in a holy place because it is a most holy part of their regular share of the offerings made to the Lord by fire."

Haggai 1:3-11 "Give careful thought to your ways. You have planted much but have harvested little. You eat but never have enough. You drink but never have your fill. You put on clothes but are not warm. You earn wages, only to put them in a purse with holes in it.' This is what the Lord Almighty says: 'Give careful thought to your ways. Go up into the mountains and bring down timber and build the house, so that I may take pleasure in it and be honored,' says the Lord. 'You expected much, but see, it turned out to be little. What you brought home, I blew away. Why?' declares the Lord Almighty. 'Because of my house, which remains a ruin, while each of you is busy with his own house.'"

If your spiritual house is not right with God and His house, then your welfare will suffer. Your home is not here, it is in heaven. People are more interested in their everyday lives, not wanting to step outside their comfort zone than in winning souls for God as we are called to do. We are all to be about our Father's business.

In tithing and giving first fruits give your best. God gave His. He died for our sins.

Malachi 3:8-10 "Will a man rob God? Yet you rob Me. But you ask, 'How do we rob you?' In tithes and offerings. You are under a curse-the whole nation of you because you are robbing me. Bring the whole tithe into the storehouse, so that there may be food in my house. 'Test Me in this,' says the Lord Almighty, 'and see if I will not throw open the floodgates of heaven and pour out so much blessing that you will not have room enough for it.'"

Luke 6:38 "Give, and it will be given to you. A good measure, pressed down, shaken together, and running over, will be poured into your lap. For with the measure you use, it will be measured to you."

Ezekiel 44:30-31 "The best of all the first fruits and of all your special gifts will belong to the priests. You are to give them the first portion of your ground meal so that a blessing may rest on your household. The priests must not eat anything, bird or animal, found dead or torn by wild animals."

When you tithe, you are giving to God. You are called to go to Church and give your tithes to the church the food talked about here is the money to keep the church going. God sees what you give and knows your heart. He knows what you give from a sincere heart. As long as you give to the church you are obeying God. What they do with it, they will have to answer to God. Make sure God's temple, is first. Make sure it is in order and then God will take care of everything else.

Matthew 6:33 "But seek first His kingdom and His righteousness, and all these things will be given to you as well."

Plunder From The Enemy

Exodus 3:21-22 "And I will make the Egyptians favorably disposed toward this people so that when you leave you will not go empty-handed. And so, you will plunder the Egyptians."

As you cross over from a life of sin to eternal life in Jesus Christ as a child of God and as you grow in your Christian walk, the trials that come your way and that you have been through will aid your devotion to God. So, in coming to God, you will not be "empty-handed." You will come to Him with faith, love, devotion, submissive obedient heart, and a heart full of gratitude for the freedom and deliverance that you now have. Praise God!

The more you have to be forgiven for the more love and devotion you will have for God.

Luke 7:41-43 "Two men owed money to a certain moneylender. One owed him five hundred denarii, and the other fifty. Neither of them had the money to pay him back, so he canceled the debts of both. Now which of them will love him more?' Simon replied, 'I suppose the one who had the bigger debt canceled."

As you go through many trials as a Christian and the certain attacks that come at you from Satan through financial trouble, unsaved loved ones or friends, emotional and health troubles, etc. These trials will actually be a blessing. God loves you and will not let anything bad happen to you. Everything that He permits will be for your good. Do you think that He would send His One and Only Son to die for your sins and then not protect you?

Romans 8:28 "And we know that in all things God works for the good of those who love Him, who have been called according to His purpose."

Everything works for your good. These trials will produce in you the godly character God wants you to have.

James 1:2-4 "Consider it pure joy, my brothers, whenever you face trials of many kinds because you know that the testing of your faith develops perseverance. Perseverance must finish its work so that you may be mature and complete, not lacking anything."

1 Peter 1:6-7 "In this you greatly rejoice, though now for a little while you may have to suffer grief in all kinds of trials. These have come so that your faith - of greater worth than gold, which perishes even though refined by fire - may be proved genuine and may result in praise, glory, and honor when Jesus Christ is revealed."

2 Peter 1:5-8 "For this very reason, make every effort to add to your faith goodness; and to goodness, knowledge; and to knowledge, self-control; and to self-control, perseverance; and to perseverance, godliness; and to godliness, brotherly kindness; and to brotherly kindness, love. For if you possess these qualities in increasing measure, they will keep you from being ineffective and unproductive in your knowledge of our Lord Jesus Christ."

Satan is actually helping you to grow as a Christian with the attacks that he throws your way. God will go with you and protect you as you go through them.

Deuteronomy 31:6 "He will never leave you nor forsake you."

Not only will He go with you, but He will also provide a way out when it gets too much to bear.

1 Corinthians 10:12-13 "So, if you think you are standing firm, be careful that you don't fall! No temptation has seized you except what is common to man. And God is faithful; He will not let you be tempted beyond what you can bear. But when you are tempted, He will also provide a way out so that you can stand up under it."

God will also protect you as you go through your trials.

Isaiah 43:1-3 "Fear not, For I have redeemed you; I have summoned you by name; you are mine. When you pass through the waters, I will be with you; and when you pass through the rivers, they will not sweep over you. When you walk through the fire, you will not be burned; the flames will not set you ablaze. For I am the Lord, your God, the Holy One of Israel, your Savior."

Not only will God be with you, protect you, and provide a way out, but nothing can take you away from Him as you go through these trials. Praise God!

John 10:27-28 "My sheep listen to My voice; I know them, and they follow Me. I give them eternal life, and they shall never perish; no one can snatch them out of My hand."

Neither can anything separate you from the love of God even if you fail or get discouraged along the way!

Romans 8:35-39 "Who shall separate us from the love of Christ? Shall trouble or hardship or persecution or famine or nakedness or danger or sword? As it is written: 'For your sake, we face death all day long; we are considered a sheep to be slaughtered.' No, in all these things we are more than conquerors through Him who loved us. For I am convinced that neither death nor life, neither angels nor demons, neither the present nor the future, nor any powers, neither height nor depth nor anything else in all creation will be able to separate us from the love of God that is in Christ Jesus our Lord."

So praise God through your trials! He will get you through victoriously and as a stronger, more faithful, mature Christian! One that He can use to further His Kingdom.

John 16:33 "I have told you these things, so that in me you may have peace. In this world, you will have trouble. But take heart! I have overcome the world."

Worship: A Pleasing Aroma To God

Genesis 8:21 "The Lord smelled the pleasing aroma and said in His heart: 'Never again will I curse the ground because of man, even though every inclination of his heart is evil from childhood. And never again will I destroy all living creatures, as I have done.'"

God does not want worship that is a lot of show and no heart. Just as described in Matthew 6:5, "And when you pray, do not be like the hypocrites, for they love to pray standing in the synagogues and on the street corners to be seen by men. I tell you the truth; they have received their reward in full." This passage talks about how you pray, but it goes for all things concerning God, your prayer life, and your worship. Things done for the show and praise of men will be your reward. There will be none from God when the focus of your worship and prayer life is for everyone else to see how holy you are. That is self-centered worship giving you the praise and glory and not God.

Isaiah 42:8 "I am the Lord; that is my name! I will not give my glory to another or my praise to idols."

Philippians 2:3 "Do nothing out of selfish ambition or vain conceit, but in humility consider others better than yourselves."

Your worship, the songs that you sing, the praise from your lips, the way that you live and as you obey God's Word must be sincere; it must be straight from the heart with a true, sincere devotion to God. It must be because you love Him and not because everyone else is doing it or because you think God will be pleased if you do it with an attitude of something you have to do. Praise pleases God when it is done in the right attitude, to please Him because you love Him and He is worthy of all praise!

John 4:24 "God is Spirit, and His worshipers must worship in spirit and in truth."

Romans 12:9-10 "Love must be sincere. Hate what is evil; cling to what is good. Be devoted to one another in brotherly love. Honor one another above yourselves."

Hebrews 10:22 "Let us draw near to God with a sincere heart full of assurance of faith, having our hearts sprinkled to cleanse us from a guilty conscience and having our bodies washed with pure water."

True worship is pleasing to God. True worship cannot contain itself. It shows you no matter what you are going through, no matter what trials and overwhelming circumstances that you are facing, you worship God because of Who HE is and the salvation that is yours through the blood of Jesus! True worship shows itself as heart-felt worship straight from the heart and it cannot be contained.

Matthew 5:14-15 "You are the light of the world. A city on a hill cannot be hidden. Neither do people light a lamp and put it under a bowl. Instead, they put it on its stand, and it gives light to everyone in the house."

Luke 6:45 "For out of the overflow of his heart his mouth speaks."

Luke 7:35 "But wisdom is proved right by all her children."

John 3:20 "For God is greater than our hearts, and He knows everything. Dear friends, if our hearts do not condemn us, we have confidence before God and receive from Him anything we ask, because we obey His commands and do what pleases Him."

As Christians, you will go through many trials. These trials are to increase your faith and help you to grow and mature spiritually and be able to withstand the fiery darts of Satan because you allow Jesus Christ to live and work big in you.

James 1:2-4 "Consider it pure joy, my brothers, whenever you face trials of many kinds because you know that the testing of your faith develops perseverance. Perseverance must finish its work so that you may be mature and complete, not lacking anything."

1 Peter 1:6-7 "In this you greatly rejoice, though now for a little while you may have had to suffer grief in all kinds of trials. These have come so that your faith - of greater worth than gold, which perishes even though refined by fire - may be proven genuine and may result in praise, glory, and honor when Jesus Christ is revealed."

Sincere love and devotion to God will radiate through you in your worship and everyday lifestyle despite going through trials and the fiery darts of Satan. Worshiping God is not only in how you praise Him in song, but you worship Him in how you live as well. How you live shows that you delight yourself in the Lord. Sincere worship is rewarded. Despite the trials you are suffering through, sincere devotion to God will radiate through you and be a witness to others.

Psalm 37:4 "Delight yourself in the Lord and He will give you the desires of your heart."

1 Thessalonians 1:6-8 "You became imitators of us and of the Lord; despite severe suffering, you welcomed the message with the joy given by the Holy Spirit. And so you became a model to all the believers in Macedonia and Achaia. The Lord's message rang out from you not only in Macedonia and Achaia - your faith in God has become known everywhere."

John 14:21 "Whoever has my commands and obeys them, he is the one who loves me. He who loves me will be loved by My Father, and I too will love him and show myself to him."

This kind of worship is pleasing to God. It shows a sincere faith. It tells Him that you love Him for Who He is and that you appreciate Him. It tells Him that you love Him for all of Who He is; you're Most High God, your heavenly Father, your Provider, and your Savior. Not just for what He can do for you. This kind of love is perfected through the fire of affliction; through the trials you go through and is still evident to all; like smoke from a fire, it is a sweet aroma that is pleasing to God. This kind of faith, love, and devotion will bring about your deliverance from God because you are seeking all of Him, not just His rewards.

Exodus 29:18 "Then burn the entire ram on the altar. It is a burnt offering to the Lord, a pleasing aroma, and an offering made to the Lord by fire."

Leviticus 1:9 "It is a burnt offering, an offering made by fire, an aroma pleasing to the Lord."

True worship will radiate straight from your heart. It starts from within and will reflect outward and not only is it pleasing to God, but it is an awesome witness to those around you.

Proverbs 27:19 "As water reflects a face, so a man's heart reflects the man."

In seeking deliverance from the hell that you are going through; you need to seek the deliverer. Jesus is the light of the world, where HE is there is no darkness! When He comes into a church, a heart, a home, and a circumstance that you are dealing with your family, all darkness must leave! So, seek Jesus, seek the deliverer! Not just deliverance! He'll deliver you from all of your problems; even ones you did not know that you had! When the light comes, the darkness has to leave!

Psalm 139:11-12 "If I say, 'Surely the darkness will hide me and the light become night around me,' even the darkness will not be dark to you; the night will shine like the day, for darkness is as light to you."

Jeremiah 29:11-14 "For I know the plans I have for you, declares the Lord, plans to prosper you and not to harm you, plans to give you hope and a future. Then you will call upon Me and come and pray to Me, and I will listen to you. You will seek Me and find Me when you seek Me with all your heart. I will be found by you, declares the Lord, and bring you back from captivity."

John 8:12 "I am the light of the world. Whoever follows me will never walk in darkness but will have the light of life."

When the woman with the alabaster box washed the Lord's feet with her tears and anointed them with expensive perfume, this pleased Jesus. We are to give Jesus our best worship! He deserves it! He died for us! Do you want to please Him? Then give Him your best in everything you do. For the glory of God! His blessings will automatically overflow into your life. He will want to bless you as He did for her.

Matthew 26:10-13 "Aware of this, Jesus said to them, 'Why are you bothering this woman? She has done a beautiful thing to me. The poor you will always have with you, but you will not always have me. When she poured this perfume on my body, she did it to prepare me for burial. I tell you the truth, wherever this gospel is preached throughout the world, what she has done will also be told, in memory of her.'"

Luke 7:37-38 "When a woman who had lived a sinful life in that town learned that Jesus was eating at the Pharisee's house, she brought an alabaster jar of perfume, and as she stood behind Him at His feet weeping, she began to wet His feet with her tears. Then she wiped them with her hair, kissed them, and poured perfume on them."

During those times that perfume was costly. We have freedom from sin and hell because of Jesus. Our sins cost Him suffering, brutal beatings, ridicule, and death on the cross.

Isaiah 52:13-15 "See my Servant will act wisely; He will be raised and lifted up and highly exalted. Just as there were many who were appalled at Him - His appearance was so disfigured beyond that of any man and His form marred beyond human likeness - so will He sprinkle many nations, and kings will shut their mouths because of Him."

What cost are you willing to pay; to go through for Him to be a witness to the world? Or do you expect everything to be handed to you on a silver platter? Life does not work that way. Jesus died for you. What are you willing to go through for Him that He may be glorified; which increases your faith and devotion because of it? Are you truly seeking Jesus? What are you doing for Him? Or are you just living for the moment and yourself and you do not care who or what you hurt in the process? He died that you might have life and have it more abundantly. He died to free you from the bondage of sin. He died that by His wounds, you would be healed. He died to give you peace and joy. He died that He would always be with you. He died for the forgiveness of your sins. As He hung on the cross He thought of you.

Luke 23:34 "Father, forgive them, for they do not know what they are doing."

What are you doing for Him?

Is the relationship that you are seeking with Jesus one-sided and selfish? Do you only want Him because of what He can bless you with? You will not find Jesus that way, nor will you find blessings. Jesus carried the cross of death and hell for us. What cross are you carrying to find true love for Him? Isn't HE worth it? I think so. His blessings far outweigh the cross we must carry. He loves you and will not hurt or abandon you. Place your love and trust in Jesus, seek Him alone and He will deliver you from all your troubles.

Deuteronomy 31:6 "He will never leave you nor forsake you."

Psalm 34:17-20 "The righteous cry out, and the Lord hears them; He delivers them from all their troubles. The Lord is close to the brokenhearted and saves those who are crushed in spirit. A righteous man may have many troubles, but the Lord delivers him from them all; He protects all his bones, not one of them will be broken."

Luke 9:23-24 "If anyone would come after me, he must deny himself and take up his cross daily and follow me. For whoever wants to save his life will lose it, but whoever loses his life for me will save it."

He will heal all your hurts. He loves you. Humble yourself and repent. Come back to Him. His arms are wide open, He will forgive you and restore you.

Isaiah 55:6-7 "Seek the Lord while He may be found; call on Him while He is near. Let the wicked forsake his way and the evil man his thoughts. Let him turn to the Lord, and He will have mercy on him, and to our God, for He will freely pardon."

When you find true love for God and praise and worship Him in all sincerity, you will find Jesus. When you do this and truly get your praise on, Satan's demons will have to go! They do not want to stick around where there is love and praise for Jesus going on!

Put on the true *garment of praise* and seek the deliverer! Satan will flee!

Isaiah 35:4 "Be strong, do not fear; your God will come, He will come with vengeance; with divine retribution He will come to save you."

What kind of praise and worship for God is in your alabaster box?

Tithing Part Of Obedience & Leads To Blessings

1 **Samuel 15:22** "To obey is better than sacrifice, and to heed is better than the fat of rams."

Tithing is also something that we are commanded to do but more importantly, by tithing you become a part of everything within the Church. By that, I mean every soul saved, everyone healed, and everyone encouraged or provided for in some way you become a partner with the Church in bringing that to pass! You cannot be everywhere at once, but tithing makes that possible. The money you give helps keep the Church operating and therefore makes you a participant in everything that happens. You may not have a voice to sing or the calling to preach but with your tithe, you become a part of it. "I thank my God every time I remember you. In all my prayers for all of you, I always pray with joy because of your partnership," (Philippians 1:3-5).

God created the world and everything in it belongs to Him. "To the Lord your God belong the heavens, even the highest heavens, the earth and everything in it," (Deuteronomy 10:14). In tithing we are becoming partners of the ministry in which we give to. So, whether we physically give of ourselves or just in our monetary donations, we are a part of every aspect of that ministry. Tithing and giving offerings and first fruits is not a work that we do, it is a heart thing. Yes, our tithes are to be 10% of our pay but we are not to look at it as something we have to do. Instead, look at it as a way to help further the kingdom of God. Life on earth is only temporary and eternity is forever. When we give, we help the ministry or Church we are giving to, to win souls, provide council, physical needs, discipleship, and love to all those who need it. When we give, we become a part of the kingdom of God's growth process and when you look at it that way it becomes a pure joy to give!

2 Corinthians 9:7-8 "Each man should give what he has decided in his heart to give, not reluctantly or under compulsion, for God loves a cheerful giver. And God is able to make all grace abound to you, so that in all things at all times, having all that you need, you will abound in every good work."

We do not give to get, but out of our love for God. When we give out of a joyful heart that is when we are blessed by God.

Proverbs 11:25 "A generous man will prosper; he who refreshes others will himself be refreshed."

Isaiah 30:23 "He will also send you rain for the seed you sow in the ground, and the food that comes from the land will be rich and plentiful."

1 Corinthians 9:10 "When the plowman plows and the thresher threshes, they ought to do so in the hope of sharing in the harvest."

2 Corinthians 9:10-11 "Now He who supplies seed to the sower and bread for food will also supply and increase your store of seed and will enlarge the harvest of your righteousness. You will be made rich in every way so that you can be generous on every occasion, and through us, your generosity will result in thanksgiving to God."

Philippians 1:4-5 "I always pray with joy because of your partnership in the gospel from the first day until now."

Our life here is but a breath.

Psalm 144:4 "Man is like a breath; his days are like a fleeting shadow."

Our goal here is to work toward our heavenly home and help the Lord bring into the family of God as many souls as possible.

Matthew 24:14 "And this gospel of the kingdom will be preached in the whole world as a testimony to all nations, and then the end will come."

Philippians 3:13-14 "Forgetting what is behind and straining toward what is ahead, I press on toward the goal to win the prize for which God has called me heavenward in Christ Jesus."

There are different ways of tithing.

1. Regular Weekly etc. or however you get paid, which is according to your regular paychecks.

Leviticus 24:8-9 "This bread is to be set out before the Lord regularly, Sabbath after Sabbath, on behalf of the Israelites, as a lasting covenant. It belongs to Aaron and his sons, who are to eat it in a holy place because it is a most holy part of their regular share of the offerings made to the Lord by fire."

Leviticus 27:30 "A tithe of the herd and flock - every tenth animal that passes under the shepherd's rod - will be holy to the Lord."

Numbers 18:21-24 "I give to the Levites all the tithes in Israel as their inheritance in return for the work they do while serving at the Tent of Meeting. From now on the Israelites must not go near the Tent of Meeting, or they will bear the consequences of their sin and will die. It is the Levites who are to do the work at the Tent of Meeting and bear the responsibility for offenses against it. This is a lasting ordinance for generations to come. They will receive no inheritance among the Israelites. Instead, I give to the Levites as their inheritance the tithes that the Israelites present as an offering to the Lord.”

Deuteronomy 18:3-5 “This is the share due the priests from the people who sacrifice a bull or a sheep: the shoulder, the jowls, and the inner parts. You are to give them the first fruits of your grain, new wine and oil, and the first wool from the shearing of your sheep, for the Lord your God has chosen them and their descendants out of all your tribes to stand and minister in the Lord’s name always.”

2. Annual Tithe: A tithe that you give at the start of every New Year. Starting the year off putting God first, will direct the rest of your year.

Proverbs 3:9-10 “Honor the Lord with your wealth, with the first fruits of all your crops; then your barns will be filled to overflowing, and your vats will brim over with new wine.”

Deuteronomy 14:22-23 “Be sure to set aside a tenth of all that your fields produce each year. Eat the tithe of your grain, new wine and oil, and the firstborn of your herds and flocks in the presence of the Lord your God at the place He will choose as a dwelling for His Name, so that you may learn to revere the Lord your God always.”

Nehemiah 10:35-37 “We also assume the responsibility for bringing to the house of the Lord each year the first fruits of our crops and of every fruit tree. As it is also written in the Law, we will bring the firstborn of our sons and of our cattle, of our herds and of our flocks to the house of our God, to the priests ministering there. Moreover, we will bring to the storerooms of the house of our God, to the priests, the first of our ground meal, of our grain offerings, of the fruit of all our trees, and of our new wine and oil. And we will bring a tithe of our crops to the Levites, for it is the Levites who collect the tithes in all the towns where we work."

Conditions of annual tithes

Every third year the tithe is to go directly to the Levites and to the poor.

Deuteronomy 26:12 "When you have finished setting aside a tenth of all your produce in the third year, the year of the tithe, you shall give it to the Levite, the alien, the fatherless and the widow, so that they may eat in your towns and be satisfied."

Deuteronomy 14:27-29 "And do not neglect the Levites living in your towns, for they have no allotment or inheritance of their own. At the end of every three years, bring all the tithes of that year's produce and store it in your towns, so that the Levites (who have no allotment or inheritance of their own) and the aliens, the fatherless and the widows who live in your towns may come and eat and be satisfied, and so that the Lord your God may bless you in all the work of your hands."

Proverbs 28:27 "He who gives to the poor will lack nothing, but he who closes his eyes to them receives many curses."

When you give, do it in all sincerity and in love.

It may be in food, clothing, housing needs, or money. In everything, give in love and with a cheerful heart.

Matthew 7:12 "So in everything, do to others what you would have them do to you."

Matthew 25:40 "I tell you the truth, whatever you did for one of the least of these brothers of mine, you did for me."

2 Corinthians 9:7-8 "Each man should give what he has decided in his heart to give, not reluctantly or under compulsion, for God loves a cheerful giver. And God is able to make all grace abound to you, so that in all things at all times, having all that you need, you will abound in every good work."

John 3:17-18 "If anyone has material possessions and sees his brother in need but has no pity on him, how can the love of God be in him? Dear children, let us not love with words or tongue but with actions and in truth."

First fruits

Honoring God with your first fruits; your heart and soul, time possessions, or money, shows that you are placing God first.

Proverbs 3:9 "Honor the Lord with thy substance, and with the first fruits of all thine increase."

Deuteronomy 26:1-4 "When you have entered the land the Lord your God is giving you as an inheritance and have taken possession of it and settled in it, take some of the first fruits of all that you produce from the soil of the land the Lord your God is giving you and put them in a basket. Then go to the place the Lord your God will choose as a dwelling for His Name and say to the priest in office at the time, 'I declare today to the Lord your God that I have come to the land the Lord swore to our forefathers to give us.' The priests shall take the basket from your hands and set it down in front of the altar of the Lord your God."

Romans 11:16 "If the part of the dough offered as first fruits is holy, then the whole batch is holy; if the root is holy, so are the branches."

1 Peter 1:16 "Be holy, because I am holy."

Proverbs 16:2 "Commit to the Lord whatever you do, and your plans will succeed."

In tithing, you are giving to God.

Give with a sincere heart in true love and devotion to God; it is an act of *worship*. How you give and how much is a symbol of where your heart really lies with God. You must give to God out of a sincere heart, knowing that in giving it is an act of obedience and worship. When you do you will give your best and will be rewarded for it.

2 Corinthians 9:12-15 "This service that you perform is not only supplying the needs of God's people but is also overflowing in many expressions of thanks to God. Because of the service by which you have proved yourselves, men will praise God for the obedience that accompanies your confession of the gospel of Christ, and for your generosity in sharing with them and with everyone else. And in their prayers for you, their hearts will go out to you, because of the surpassing grace God has given you. Thanks be to God for His indescribable gift."

Psalm 100:4 "Enter His gates with thanksgiving and His courts with praise; give thanks to Him and praise His name."

Malachi 3:10-12 "Bring the whole tithe into the storehouse, that there may be food in MY house. Test Me in this,' says the Lord Almighty, 'and see if I will not throw open the floodgates of heaven and pour out so much blessing that you will not have room enough for it.

I will prevent pests from devouring your crops, and the vines in your fields will not cast their fruit,' says the Lord Almighty. 'Then all the nations will call you blessed, for yours will be a delightful land,' says the Lord Almighty."

Jeremiah 17:10 "I the Lord search the heart and examine the mind, to reward a man according to his conduct, according to what his deeds deserve."

Luke 6:38 "Give and it will be given to you. A good measure, pressed down, shaken together, and running over, will be poured into your lap. For with the measure you use, it will be measured to you."

God is the One who directs our steps and those all around us. He is the One who supplies all of our needs. Trust Him to take care of your needs as you help to take care of the needs of the church and of those in need around you.

James 4:17 "Anyone, then, who knows the good he ought to do and doesn't do it, sins."

.

Romans 12:13 "Share with God's people who are in need. Practice hospitality."

Philippians 4:19 "And my God will meet all your needs according to His glorious riches in Christ Jesus."

Psalm 55:22 "Cast all your cares on the Lord and He will sustain you; He will never let the righteous fall."

Examine your heart as you give to God to see if your giving is truly an act of love, devotion, and sincere worship. Do you trust Him to supply all your needs as you give your best or do you hold back in fear? Are you scared God will not come through for you? Fear is not from God.

Deuteronomy 31:6 "Be strong and courageous. Do not be afraid or terrified because of them for the Lord your God goes with you; He will never leave you nor forsake you."

Romans 8:15 "For you did not receive a spirit that makes you a slave again to fear, but you received the Spirit of sonship. And by Him, we cry Abba, Father."

Remember the verse in Malachi; the Lord says, "Test *me*." If you are scared your bills will not be met, test God in this and see, do it afraid. It will break the chains of fear as you tithe and give from the heart, listening to God's still small voice directing you, when he comes through for you in a *big* way! He does everything for the glory of His name and wants you to trust Him. The world and everything in it are His and He gives it to anyone He pleases. We serve a big God and He is not poor!

Example: If you have a hundred dollars in your wallet and you only give $1.00, where then is your heart and your trust in God to provide all your needs? If you have plenty of free time and fill it with TV, other books or games, etc., and leave reading the Bible totally out of your day, where then is your love and devotion to God really at?

John 4:24 "God is spirit, and His worshipers must worship in spirit and in truth."

Matthew 6:19-21 "Do not store up for yourselves treasures on earth, where moth and rust destroy, and where thieves break in and steal. But store up for yourselves treasures in heaven, where moth and rust do not destroy, and where thieves do not break in and steal. For where your treasure is, there your heart will be also."

Matthew 6:24 "No one can serve two masters. Either he will hate the one and love the other, or he will be devoted to the one and despise the other. You cannot serve both God and Money."

2 Corinthians 9:6 "Remember this: Whoever sows sparingly will also reap sparingly, and whoever sows generously will also reap generously."

Proverbs 21:2 "All of man's ways seem right to him, but the Lord weighs the heart."

Pray about the first fruits of the year.

The first fruits of the year are something that you must pray about on how and how much to give. Give it all at once if you are able or split it up. In everything seek God.

Psalm 34:10 "The lions may grow weak and hungry, but those who seek the Lord lack no good thing."

1 Thessalonians 5:16 "Be joyful always; pray continually; give thanks in all circumstances, for this is God's will for you in Christ Jesus."

Philippians 4:6 "Do not be anxious about anything, but in everything, by prayer and petition, with thanksgiving, present your requests to God."

First fruits of your regular tithe

In your regular tithe, you are to set aside a tenth (or more whatever you choose to give) of the first part of your pay. Not leftovers. God gave His best for our salvation. He gave Himself in Jesus Christ. Jesus is an awesome gift of love to us. We should give our best to Him.

Matthew 1:23 "The virgin will be with child and will give birth to a Son, and they will call Him Immanuel-which means, 'God with us."

John 3:16 "For God so loved the world that He gave His One and Only Son, that whoever believes in Him shall not perish but have eternal life."

James 1:16-18 "Don't be deceived, my dear brothers. Every good and perfect gift is from above, coming down from the Father of the heavenly lights, who does not change like shifting shadows. He chose to give us birth through the Word of truth that we might be a kind of first fruits of all He created."

Ezekiel 44:30 "The best of all the first fruits and of all your special gifts will belong to the priests. You are to give them the first portion of your ground meal so that a blessing may rest on your household."

First fruits at the start of a new year

In the first month of the start of a new year, you offer first fruits to the Lord. You can give the first week's pay of the first month of the New Year to the Lord. You can split this up throughout the month or give it all at once.

Exodus 34:22 "Celebrate the Feast of Weeks with the first fruits of the wheat harvest, and the Feast of In-gathering at the turn of the year."

First fruits can be a new job or a special gift given to you.

You can also give the first paycheck of a new job or a tenth of the value of a gift or money someone has blessed you with. After all, "every good and perfect gift is from above." God directs the steps of man and has led you to your job and blesses you with the talents that you have. Show Him true thanks and praise for it.

Proverbs 20:24 "A man's steps are directed by the Lord. How then can anyone understand his own way?"

Deuteronomy 8:18 "But remember the Lord your God, for it is He who gives you the ability to produce wealth, and so confirms His covenant, which He swore to your forefathers, as it is today."

Leviticus 23:10-11 "When you enter the land, I am going to give you and you reap its harvest, bring to the priest a sheaf of the first grain you harvest. He is to wave the sheaf before the Lord so it will be accepted on your behalf; the priest is to wave it on the day after the Sabbath."

First fruits is a gift of your heart, soul, life, and time.

Let today be the first day of the rest of your life; here on earth and in heaven. Give your heart and soul to the Lord, knowing now that your eternal home will be heaven.

John 5:11-12 "And this is the testimony: God has given us eternal life, and this life is in His Son. He who has the Son has life; he who does not have the Son of God does not have life."

Romans 8:23-24 "Not only so, but we ourselves, who have the first fruits of the Spirit, groan inwardly as we wait eagerly for our adoption as sons, the redemption of our bodies. For in this hope, we are saved."

Start your day off with time in the Word. If God can give His best; we can give ours. If for some reason you had to get up a little extra early to go to work, earlier than usual, you would get up. Wouldn't you?

Why not get up a little earlier to spend time with God? After all, He is the One who created you, He is the One who gives you breath, He is the One who blesses you and He is the One who saves you and gives you eternal life! Why not show Him a little devotion, love, and time to spend with Him? If He can die for us, can't we be a little more devoted to Him? Or is your relationship with Him all one-sided? You take.

Mark 1:35 "Very early in the morning, while it was still dark, Jesus got up, left the house, and went off to a solitary place, where He prayed."

Psalm 5:3 "In the morning, O Lord, you hear my voice; in the morning I lay my requests before you and wait in expectation."

Ecclesiastes 11:6 "Sow your seed in the morning, and at evening let not your hands be idle, for you do not know which will succeed, whether this or that, or whether both will do equally well."

Psalm 92:1-2 "It is good to praise the Lord and make music to your name, O Most High, to proclaim your love in the morning and your faithfulness at night."

Tithing or not tithing can either bring blessings or discipline. Which do you prefer?

Just as you are pleased when your own children obey, love, and trust you; so it is with God. Just as well, He is not pleased when you disobey.

Ephesians 5:6 "God's wrath comes on those who are disobedient."

What God gives, He can also take away.

Deuteronomy 28:15-20 "However, if you do not obey the Lord your God and do not carefully follow all His commands and decrees, I am giving you today, all these curses will come upon you and overtake you: You will be cursed in the city and cursed in the country. Your basket and your kneading trough will be cursed. The fruit of your womb will be cursed, and the crops of your land, and the calves of your herds, and the lambs of your flocks. You will be cursed when you come in and cursed when you go out. The Lord will send on you curses, confusion, and rebuke in everything you put your hand to until you are destroyed and come to sudden ruin because of the evil you have done in forsaking Him."

Haggai 1:3-11 "Give careful thought to your ways. You have planted much but have harvested little. You eat but never have enough. You drink but never have your fill. You put on clothes but are not warm. You earn wages, only to put them in a purse with holes in it.' This is what the Lord Almighty says, 'Give careful thought to your ways. Go up into the mountains and bring down timber and build the house, so that I may take pleasure in it and be honored,' says the Lord. 'You expected much, but see, it turned out to be little. What you brought home, I blew away. Why?' declares the Lord Almighty. 'Because of my house, which remains a ruin, while each of you is busy with his own house.'"

In tithing and giving first fruits give your best. God gave His. He died for our sins.

Exodus 23:19 "Bring the best of the first fruits of your soil to the house of the Lord your God."

Withholding from God will bring about His discipline. You reap what you sow.

Proverbs 21:13 "If a man shuts his ears to the cry of the poor, he too will cry out and not be answered."

Galatians 6:7 "Do not be deceived: God cannot be mocked. A man reaps what he sows. The one who sows to please his sinful nature, from that nature will reap destruction; the one who sows to please the Spirit, from the Spirit will reap eternal life."

Proverbs 11:24-25 "One man gives freely, yet gains even more; another withholds unduly but comes to poverty. A generous man will prosper; he who refreshes others will himself be refreshed."

Tithing as part of obedience is taking care of the pastors, preachers, and evangelists who have made serving God their whole livelihood.

Tithing is God's way of taking care of those who are daily taking care of God's Business, witnessing and saving souls.

1 Corinthians 9:10 "When the plowman plows and the thresher threshes, they ought to do so in the hope of sharing in the harvest."

Matthew 28:18-20 "All authority in heaven and on earth has been given to me. Therefore, go and make disciples of all nations, baptizing them in the name of the Father and of the Son and of the Holy Spirit, and teaching them to obey everything I have commanded you. And surely, I am with you always, to the very end of the age."

Mark 16:15 "Go into all the world and preach the good news to all creation."

This is how God provides their salary and the overhead costs of running His church and for the provision of outreach ministries within the church. We witness and have secular jobs. Witnessing is their job, their life.

1 Corinthians 9:14 "In the same way, the Lord has commanded that those who preach the gospel should receive their living from the gospel."

When we give, we are giving to God. What God does with it is His business.

Malachi 3:8-10 "Will a man rob God? Yet you rob Me.' But you ask, 'How do we rob you?' 'In tithes and offerings. You are under a curse - the whole nation of you - because you are robbing ME. Bring the whole tithe into the storehouse, that there may be food in MY house. Test Me in this,' says the Lord Almighty, 'and see if I will not throw open the floodgates of heaven and pour out so much blessing that you will not have room enough for it."

Jeremiah 27:5 "With My great power and outstretched arm I made the earth and its people and the animals that are on it, and I give it to anyone I please."
If they misuse what the Lord supplies to them it is their responsibility. If they misuse it out of no respect for the Lord, they will answer for it.

Numbers 18:23 "It is the Levites who are to do the work at the Tent of Meeting and bear the responsibility for offenses against it."

One example of this is with the sons of Eli. The High Priest of Israel in 930 BC. His two sons had no respect for the Lord.

1 Samuel 2:12 "Eli's sons were wicked men; they had no regard for the Lord."

1 Samuel 2:17 "The sin of the young men was very great in the Lord's sight, for they were treating the Lord's offering with contempt."

They handled the burnt offerings with no respect. It was the Lord's will that they be put to death.

1 Samuel 2:25 "If a man sins against another man, God may mediate for him; but if a man sins against the Lord, who will intercede for him? His sons, however, did not listen to their father's rebuke, for it was the Lord's will to put them to death."

Today whether it is physically or spiritually, the outcome of death is the same, separation from God and His blessings. Salvation is eternal joy and peace. God gave us His best in Jesus Christ. He took our punishment, which was an act of total unselfishness and an act of an abounding sacrificial love. The very least we can do is to tithe and to give our best in it. When you think about it, holding out on God is selfish. It is putting our needs before His. How can we do that when He died for us? He gives us the breath of life and directs our steps to the jobs that we have. He supplies our needs in the home, clothing, and food that we have.

We are to sow our seed into good soil, so search your heart in the church that you go to and the other ministries that you want to give an offering to, to make sure it is good soil.   Pastors and evangelists that have received God's whole Word and believe it; teach it, and practice is good soil. They understand God's will and His Word and obey it.

Matthew 13:23 "But the one who received the seed that fell on good soil is the man who hears the word and understands it."

Matthew 6:33 "But seek first His kingdom and His righteousness, and all these things will be given to you as well."

He answers our prayers and showers blessing upon blessing down on us. Because of Him, we will have an eternity in heaven; eternal peace and joy.

Revelation 21:4 "He will wipe every tear from their eyes. There will be no more death or mourning or crying or pain, for the old order of things has passed away."

He died for the sins of all mankind while we were still sinning against Him. He took beatings for us.

Isaiah 52:14 "Just as there were many who were appalled at Him - His appearance was so disfigured beyond that of any man and His form marred beyond human likeness."

Romans 5:8 "But God demonstrates His own love for us in this: While we were still sinners, Christ died for us."

1 Corinthians 15:20-22 "But Christ has indeed been raised from the dead, the first fruits of those who have fallen asleep. For since death came through a man, the resurrection of the dead comes also through a man. For as in Adam all die, so in Christ all will be made alive."

Give the best of your heart, soul, and life to God.

Give Him the best of your time, service, and money.

Matthew 22:37-38 "Love the Lord your God with all your heart and with all your soul and with all your mind. This is the first and greatest commandment."

Matthew 16:26-27 "What good will it be for a man if he gains the whole world, yet forfeits his soul? For the Son of Man is going to come in His Father's glory with His angels, and then He will reward each person according to what he has done."

We Are Blessed In Jesus Christ!

Ephesians 1:3 "Praise be to the God and Father of our Lord Jesus Christ, who has blessed us in the heavenly realms with every spiritual blessing in Christ."

Jesus is Every Spiritual Blessing that we need.

Every spiritual blessing is ours! In this world, you will have trials. Jesus had trials and you are not above Him that you should be exempt from them. But He does promise us every spiritual blessing through God the Father and Himself! If you need comfort, encouragement, strength, protection, love, wisdom, peace, and joy, or a helping hand to endure the trial that you are going through all you have to do is ask! Whatever the need, Jesus is the answer. All you have to do to receive is ask.

Psalm 28:8 "The Lord is the strength of His people, a fortress of salvation for His anointed one."

Psalm 29:11 "The Lord gives strength to His people; the Lord blesses His people with peace."

Psalm 32:7 "You are my hiding place; you will protect me from trouble and surround me with songs of deliverance."

Psalm 34:4 "I sought the Lord, and He answered me; He delivered me from all my fears."

Psalm 34:17-20 "The righteous cry out, and the Lord hears them; He delivers them from all their troubles. The Lord is close to the brokenhearted and saves those who are crushed in spirit. A righteous man may have many troubles, but the Lord delivers him from them all; He protects all his bones, not one of them will be broken."

Proverbs 18:10 "The name of the Lord is a strong tower; the righteous run to it and are safe."

John 14:27 "Peace I leave with you; my peace I give you. I do not give to you as the world gives. Do not let your hearts be troubled and do not be afraid."

Romans 8:15-16 "For you did not receive a spirit that makes you a slave again to fear, but you received the Spirit of sonship. And by Him, we cry, '*Abba.*' Father. The Spirit Himself testifies with our spirit that we are God's children."

2 Corinthians 1:3-4 "Praise be to the God and Father of our Lord Jesus Christ, the Father of compassion and the God of all comfort, who comforts us in all our troubles so that we can comfort those in any trouble with the comfort we ourselves have received from God."

Galatians 5:22-23 But the fruit of the Spirit is love, joy, peace, patience, kindness, goodness, faithfulness, gentleness and self-control."

Ephesians 2:14-15 "For He Himself is our peace, who has made the two one and has destroyed the barrier, the dividing wall of hostility, by abolishing in His flesh the law with its commandments and regulations."

Philippians 4:13 "I can do everything through Him who gives me strength."

James 1:5 "If any of you lacks wisdom, he should ask God, who gives generously to all without finding fault, and it will be given to him."

James 4:2 "You do not have, because you do not ask God."

Whatever you need, in Christ you already have it!

John 14:6 "I am the way and the truth and the life. No one comes to the Father except through me."

Whatever you need, that is what He is to you.

Exodus 3:14 "God said to Moses, 'I Am Who I Am. This is what you are to say to the Israelites: I Am has sent me to you."

Jesus is there for us in our trials.

We all have trials to go through that seem to us as if the world is caving in all around us. Don't think that you are going it alone. God will never leave you alone.

Deuteronomy 31:6 "Be strong and courageous. Do not be afraid or terrified because of them, for the Lord your God goes with you; He will never leave you nor forsake you."

Nothing can separate you from God's love. Even when you stumble and your faith takes a nosedive or you sin as you go through your trials, God is a merciful and compassionate God. If He loved you enough to die for you, then you know that He loves you enough to pick you back up when you fall.

Psalm 145:18 "The Lord is near to all who call on Him, to all who call on Him in truth."

Romans 8:37-39 "No, in all these things we are more than conquerors through Him who loved us. For I am convinced that neither death nor life, neither angels nor demons, neither the present nor the future, nor any powers, neither height nor depth nor anything else in all creation, will be able to separate us from the love of God that is in Christ Jesus our Lord."

The Lord will guide you, go with you, and protect you through your trials as you trust in Him. He will also restore your heart and soul when the going gets a little rough and He will bless you abundantly. Psalm 23 tells you all of this.

Psalm 23 "The Lord is my Shepherd; I shall not be in want. He makes me lie down in green pastures, He leads me beside quiet waters, and he restores my soul. He guides me in paths of righteousness for His name's sake. Even though I walk through the valley of the shadow of death, I will fear no evil, for you are with me; your rod and your staff, they comfort me. You prepare a table before me in the presence of my enemies. You anoint my head with oil and my cup overflows. Surely goodness and love will follow me all the days of my life, and I will dwell in the house of the Lord forever."

Jesus provides what you need to get you through trials.

The problems that come your way, your emotional or health problems, family, job, or financial problems; whatever it is, God didn't send it. He is a God of love. But He will use it for your good.

John 4:16 "And so we know and rely on the love God has for us. God is love."

Romans 8:28 "And we know that in all things God works for the good of those who love Him, who have been called according to His purpose."

God will use everything that comes your way, either from Satan or your own bad choices, for your good. To mold you and draw you closer to Him. To strengthen you and help your faith and trust in Him to grow. What Satan means for bad, God will use for good. Not everything is from Satan either; some are from your own carnal nature; your own bad choices. We all have choices to make either good or bad. The choice is yours and so are the consequences.

Deuteronomy 30:19-20 "This day I call heaven and earth as witnesses against you that I have set before you life and death, blessings and curses. Now choose life, so that you and your children may live and that you may love the Lord your God, listen to His voice, and hold fast to Him. For the Lord is your life, and He will give you many years in the land He swore to give to your fathers, Abraham, Isaac, and Jacob."

Galatians 5:16-17 "So I say, live by the Spirit, and you will not gratify the desires of the sinful nature. For the sinful nature desires what is contrary to the Spirit, and the Spirit what is contrary to the sinful nature."

Galatians 6:7-8 "A man reaps what he sows. The one who sows to please his sinful nature, from that nature will reap destruction; the one who sows to please the Spirit, from the Spirit will reap eternal life."

God loves you so much that He has made every spiritual blessing available to you through Jesus Christ! You can't fail if you are a child of God. Some of these blessings are His mercy and compassion.

Lamentations 3:22-24 "Because of the Lord's great love we are not consumed, for His compassion never fail. They are new every morning; great is your faithfulness. I say to myself, 'The Lord is my portion; therefore I will wait for Him.'"

Romans 15-16 "I will have mercy on whom I will have mercy, and I will have compassion on whom I will have compassion. It does not, therefore, depend on man's desire or effort, but on God's mercy."

Whenever we take our eyes off Jesus and of following His example, we fall; we sin.

John 13:15 "I have set you an example that you should do as I have done for you."

We are to fix our eyes on Jesus, read the Word, and obey it; it will strengthen us and give us the power to say *no* to ungodliness.

Romans 10:17 "Consequently, faith comes from hearing the message, and the message is heard through the Word of Christ."

2 Corinthians 4:17-18 "For our light and momentary troubles are achieving for us an eternal glory that far out weights them all. So we fix our eyes not on what is seen, but on what is unseen. For what is seen is temporary, but what is unseen is eternal."

Hebrews 12:1-3 "Therefore, since we are surrounded by such a great cloud of witnesses, let us throw off everything that hinders and the sin that so easily entangles, and let us run with perseverance the race marked out for us. Let us fix our eyes on Jesus, the author and perfecter of our faith, who for the joy set before Him endured the cross, scorning its shame, and sat down at the right hand of the throne of God. Consider Him who endured such opposition from sinful men, so that you will not grow weary and lose heart."

Titus 2:11-13 For the grace of God that brings salvation has appeared to all men. It teaches us to say "No" to ungodliness and worldly passions, and to live self-controlled, upright, and godly lives in this present age, while we wait for the blessed hope - the glorious appearing of our great God and Savior, Jesus Christ."

When Peter saw Jesus walking on the water, by faith he got out of the boat. He did something. Jesus did not take him by the hand and make him get out of the boat. He will not do that to us either. He wants us to love, follow, obey, and have faith in Him out of our own free will. A love given freely is a love that is faithful and worth having. A love forced is slavery. God promises freedom. "The Lord sets the prisoners free, the Lord gives sight to the blind." (Psalm 146:7-8). When Peter took his eyes off of Jesus as he walked on water to Him, he fell. That is what happens to all of us when we take our eyes off of Jesus and start looking at the circumstances surrounding us instead of the promise of victory that we have in Jesus. Yet, Jesus did not condemn him, He held out His hand and picked him up.

Psalm 145:14 "The Lord upholds all those who fall and lifts up all who are bowed down."

Jesus does this for us because of His overwhelming, never-ending love for us. When we start to go the wrong way He will direct our paths and make our crooked paths straight as we trust in Him and when we come to Him and ask for forgiveness and for His help. His hands are always open and waiting for us. His forgiveness is always there.

Luke 3:5-6 "Every valley shall be filled in, every mountain and hill made low. The crooked roads shall become straight, the rough ways smooth. And all mankind will see God's salvation."

John 1:8-9 "If we claim to be without sin, we deceive ourselves and the truth is not in us. If we confess our sins, He is faithful and just and will forgive us our sins and purify us from all unrighteousness."

In our weakness, God is there with His grace to make our way perfect.

Psalm 18:32 "It is God who arms me with strength and makes my way perfect."

2 Corinthians 12:8 "My grace is sufficient for you, for My power is made perfect in weakness."

When you seem all confused and need direction, where to go, what to say or do, just go to God in prayer. Ask and you will receive. God cares for you.

1 Peter 5:7 "Cast all your anxiety on Him because He cares for you."

Psalm 25:4-5 "Show me Your ways, O Lord, teach me Your paths; guide me in Your truth and teach me, for You are God my Savior, and my hope is in You all day long."

Psalm 119:105 "Your Word is a lamp to my feet and a light for my path."

Psalm 143:8-10 "Let the morning bring me word of Your unfailing love, for I have put my trust in You. Show me the way I should go, for to You I lift up my soul. Rescue me from my enemies, O Lord, for I hide myself in You. Teach me to do Your will, for You are my God; may Your good Spirit lead me on level ground."

Proverbs 20:24 "A man's steps are directed by the Lord. How then can anyone understand his own way?"

Jesus was made man and went through trials and suffered so He could understand us and be there for us in our trials and times of need.

Psalm 55:22 "Cast your cares on the Lord and He will sustain you; He will never let the righteous fall."

Psalm 145:19-20 "He fulfills the desires of those who fear Him; He hears their cry and saves them. The Lord watches over all who love Him, but all the wicked He will destroy."

Psalm 146:5-10 "Blessed is he whose help is the God of Jacob, whose hope is in the Lord his God, the Maker of heaven and earth, the sea, and everything in them - the Lord, Who remains faithful forever. He upholds the cause of the oppressed and gives food to the hungry. The Lord sets the prisoners free; the Lord gives sight to the blind, the Lord lifts up those who are bowed down, and the Lord loves the righteous. The Lord watches over the alien and sustains the fatherless and the widow, but he frustrates the ways of the wicked. The Lord reigns forever, you're God, O Zion, for all generations. Praise the Lord."

Hebrews 2:17-18 "For this reason He had to be made like His brothers in every way, in order that He might become a merciful and faithful High Priest in service to God, and that He might make atonement for the sins of the people. Because He himself suffered when He was tempted, He is able to help those who are being tempted."

Jesus is our provision in all things.

Whatever your need is, whether you are going through an overwhelming trial or just have a need, it has already been provided for you in Jesus. The fullness of God is in Jesus Christ and if you are saved by His grace and the blood He shed on Calvary, Jesus is in you. The fullness of Christ is in you as well! Every spiritual blessing is already yours! Praise God!

Ephesians 1:22-23 "And God placed all things under His feet and appointed Him to be head over everything for the church, which is His body, the fullness of Him who fills everything in every way."

Ephesians 3:16-21 "I pray that out of His glorious riches He may strengthen you with power through His Spirit in your inner being, so that Christ may dwell in your hearts through faith. And I pray that you, being rooted and established in love, may have power, together with all the saints, to grasp how wide and long and high and deep is the love of Christ, and to know this love that surpasses knowledge - that you may be filled to the measure of all the fullness of God. Now to Him Who is able to do immeasurably more than all we ask or imagine, according to His power that is at work within us, to Him be glory in the church and in Christ Jesus throughout all generations, forever and ever! Amen."

Colossians 2:9-10 "For in Christ all the fullness of the Deity lives in bodily form, and you have been given fullness in Christ, Who is the head over every power and authority."

Colossians 3:11 "Here there is no Greek or Jew, circumcised or uncircumcised, barbarian, Scythian, slave or free, but Christ is all and is in all."

Apart from Jesus, we can do nothing, but with Him all things are possible, and our victory has already been established! Praise God! All we have to do is believe this and live and act and speak as though we believe it. What would you rather believe; the victory that God says you have, or the thoughts of fear and doubt from Satan? I don't know about you, but since God created the world, the heavens, and everything in them and the created is not stronger or more powerful than its Creator, I think I would rather believe God. You just need faith, and the blessings of God are yours!!!! He has been through your trials ahead of you so, He already knows the outcome. You win!! Trust Him!

Deuteronomy 9:3 "But be assured today that the Lord your God is the One Who goes across ahead of you like a devouring fire. He will destroy them; He will subdue them before you. And you will drive them out and annihilate them quickly, as the Lord has promised you."

Proverbs 3:5-6 "Trust in the Lord with all your heart and lean not on your own understanding; in all your ways acknowledge Him, and He will make your paths straight."

When your faith is weak, God understands. Just ask for help and admit your weak faith. God appreciates your honesty.

Proverbs 12:22) "The Lord detests lying lips, but He delights in men who are truthful."

Mark 9:24 "Immediately the boy's father exclaimed, 'I do believe, help me overcome my unbelief!'"

Luke 17:5 "The apostles said to the Lord, 'Increase our faith!'"

Nothing is impossible for you when you believe God's Word and trust in Him. Ask in faith as a child of God and you will receive.

Matthew 19:26 "With man this is impossible, but with God all things are possible."

Mark 9:23 "Everything is possible for him who believes."

Hebrews 11:6 "And without faith it is impossible to please God, because anyone who comes to Him must believe that He exists and that He rewards those who earnestly seek Him."

In Christ, we have all we need to go through our trials and everyday life with our heads held high. Knowing who you are, a child of the Most High God!!!

John 1:12 "Yet to all who received Him, to those who believed in His name, He gave the right to become children of God."

Hebrews 4:16 "Let us then approach the throne of grace with confidence, so that we may receive mercy and find grace to help us in our time of need."

Hebrews 10:35-36 "So do not throw away your confidence; it will be richly rewarded. You need to persevere so that when you have done the will of God, you will receive what He has promised."

Trials are to help us grow and mature in Christ. Just as in school you have lessons, homework, and tests to help you learn the subject that you are studying.

Philippians 1:27-29 "Whatever happens, conduct ourselves in a manner worthy of the gospel of Christ. Then, whether I come and see you or only hear about you in my absence, I will know that you stand firm in one spirit, contending as one man for the faith of the gospel without being frightened in any way by those who oppose you. This is a sign to them that they will be destroyed, but that you will be saved - and that by God. For it has been granted to you on behalf of Christ not only to believe on Him, but also to suffer for Him."

James 1:2-4 "Consider it pure joy, my brothers, whenever you face trials of many kinds because you know that the testing of your faith develops perseverance. Perseverance must finish its work so that you may be mature and complete, not lacking anything."

Jesus is our blessing and our victory.

God loves you so much, He wants to bless you. Just like you want to do good things for your children, as children of God, He wants blessings for us. He understands when you need help, and He is always there for you. Trust Him.

Jeremiah 29:11 "For I know the plans I have for you,' declares the Lord, 'plans to prosper you and not to harm you, plans to give you hope and a future.'"

Psalm 18:35 "You give me your shield of victory, and your right hand sustains me; you stoop down to make me great."

Psalm 31: 19 "How great is your goodness, which you have stored up for those who fear you, which you bestow in the sight of men on those who take refuge in you."

Psalm 147:3 "He heals the brokenhearted and binds up their wounds."

Psalm 147:5 "Great is our Lord and mighty in power; His understanding has no limit."

Psalm 147:14 "He grants peace to your borders and satisfies you with the finest of wheat."

God is always watching over you. Just as you do for your own children. Just trust in His love and know that whatever comes your way, it will always end in victory!! To the praise and glory of His name, we are always the victor!! Praise God!!

Psalm 60:12 "With God we will gain the victory, and he will trample down our enemies."

1 Corinthians 15:57 "He gives us the victory through our Lord Jesus Christ."

Psalm 121 "I lift up my eyes to the hills - where does my help come from? My help comes from the Lord, the Maker of heaven and earth. He will not let your foot slip - He who watches over you will not slumber; indeed, He who watches over Israel will neither slumber nor sleep. The Lord watches over you - the Lord is your shade at your right hand; the sun will not harm you by day, nor the moon by night. The Lord will keep you from all harm - He will watch over your life; the Lord will watch over your coming and going both now and forevermore."

Every spiritual blessing is ours, *especially* victory!

Final Thoughts

I hope you have been blessed and have learned a great deal about how to walk with God and how to stand up against the attacks of the devil. God knew you before you were in your mother's womb, and He has had a plan for you all along. So, fear not! Don't let Satan make you afraid when the storms of life hit in all directions. God is always with you. "O Lord, you have searched me, and you know me. You know when I sit and when I rise; you perceive my thoughts from afar. You discern my going out and my lying down; you are familiar with all my ways. Before a word is on my tongue you know it completely, O Lord," (Psalm 139:1-4). "All the days ordained for me were written in your book before one of them came to be," (Psalm 139:16).

He already knew the mistakes you would make and the sins you would commit. He knew the same for all of mankind and He had a plan all along. "For we are God's workmanship, created in Christ Jesus to do good works, which God has prepared in advance for us to do" (Ephesians 2:10). God knows every step you take in advance. There is nothing that you do that is a surprise to Him; He knows those who are truly His, those who have stumbled and turned aside, and who will turn back to Him. Sadly enough, He also knows those who will not. "But be assured today that the Lord your God is the one who goes across ahead of you like a devouring fire. He will destroy them; He will subdue them before you. And you will drive them out and annihilate them quickly, as the Lord has promised," (Deuteronomy 9:3). He has been through ahead of you and has a plan to correct it, but you need to trust, listen, obey, and yield yourself to Him in order for His plan to be set in motion; He will correct your steps. "Every valley shall be filled in, every mountain and hill made low. The crooked roads shall become straight, the rough ways smooth. And all mankind will see God's salvation," (Luke 3:5-6).

God knew that mankind would fall; He knows the flesh is weak. "Watch and pray that you may not enter into temptation. The spirit indeed is willing, but the flesh is weak," (Mark 14:38). God had a plan all along; yes, He could have made us perfect from the beginning, but learning from mistakes and the free will to choose for your self makes the gift you receive all the more precious to you. It is the same with our own children and our husband or wife; do you want them to love you because they choose to or because you made them? Love is always true and sincere when it is given freely and that is what God wants from us and is the reason He did not make us perfect without flaws, almost like robots, from the beginning. "Let us draw near to God with a sincere heart in full assurance of faith," (Hebrews 10:22).

The Bible is the story of Jesus, and you cannot have the New without the Old Testament; you need them both. In the Old Testament, the sacrifices and the Tabernacle symbolize Jesus who is our Tabernacle, and the ultimate sacrifice He paid for our sins; He is our Mercy Seat. The Exodus, leaving Egypt—symbolizes us as we leave a life of sin to receive Jesus Christ as Lord. The battles they fought are no different from the battles, the trials of life we fight which are to weed out the impurities and grow us into mature children of God. The Old Testament teaches us of who Jesus is, the Son of God, our Savior who gave His life for us. He is the Tabernacle within our hearts when we receive Him and the sacrifice He made. "This is good and pleases God our Savior, who wants all men to be saved and to come to knowledge of the truth. For there is one God and one Mediator between God and men, the man Christ Jesus, who gave Himself as a ransom for all men—the testimony given in its proper time," (1 Timothy 2:3-6).

The Old Testament leads us to the New in which the Ten Commandments, the laws which could never be kept were to lead us to God, to Christ, and show us what sin is; knowing that without Him, we cannot keep them. "Therefore no one will be declared righteous in His sight by observing the law; rather, through the law we become conscious of sin," (Romans 3:20). Jesus is the law, and He fulfilled the law and with His Holy Spirit within us, we can keep the law by the power of His Spirit. "Therefore, there is now no condemnation for those who are in Christ Jesus because through Christ Jesus the law of the Spirit of life set me free from the law of sin and death. For what the law was powerless to do in that it was weakened by the sinful nature, God did by sending His own Son in the likeness of sinful man to be a sin offering. And so, He condemned sin in sinful man in order that the righteous requirements of the law might be fully met in us, who do not live according to the sinful nature but according to the Spirit," (Romans 8:1-4).

Through Jesus and His Holy Spirit, we are filled completely with everything we need to have a life of victory. "And God placed all things under His feet and appointed Him to be head over everything for the church, which is His body, the fullness of Him who fills everything in every way," (Ephesians 1:22-23).

The New Testament shows us what it means to be saved and how to receive it. "For all have sinned and fall short of the glory of God and are justified freely by His grace through the redemption that came by Christ Jesus. God presented Him as a sacrifice of atonement, through faith in His blood," (Romans 3:23-25). You receive it by believing in God and in Jesus His Son and the sacrifice He made, repenting of sin, and asking Him into your heart. "That if you confess with your mouth, 'Jesus is Lord,' and believe in your heart that God raised Him from the dead, you will be saved. For it is with your heart that you believe and are justified, and it is with your mouth that you confess and are saved," (Romans 10:9-10). As we are now a new creation in Christ, we are to be holy as He is holy. "But now He has reconciled you by Christ's physical body through death to present you holy in His sight, without blemish and free from accusation," (Colossians 1:22). It also is a guide to show us how to live a godly life through Jesus Christ; on our own, we can do nothing, but through Him and the power of His blood and resurrection, we can do everything! "I am the vine; you are the branches. If a man remains in me and me in him, he will bear much fruit; apart from me you can do nothing," (John 15:5). "I can do everything through Him who gives me strength," (Philippians 4:13). "But the Counselor, the Holy Spirit, whom the Father will send in My name, will teach you all things and will remind you of everything I have said to you," (John 14:26).

God had a plan all along and the awesome show of love by the sacrifice of Jesus proved it and in such a way that we should never doubt God but trust Him completely. "Dear friends, let us love one another, for love comes from God. This is how God showed His love among us: He sent His One and Only Son into the world so that we might live through Him. This is love: not that we loved God, but that He loved us and sent His Son as an atoning sacrifice for our sins" (John 4:7, 9-10). God created us and provided salvation for us so we could live with Him in heaven for an eternity. "In Him we were also chosen, having been predestined according to the plan of Him who works out everything in conformity with the purpose of His will, in order that we, who were the first to hope in Christ, might be for the praise of His glory," (Ephesians 1:11-12). He is Almighty, powerful, and more loving than any of us can really comprehend! He wants to care for us as we do for our children! Praise God, for He truly is amazing!

"Praise be to the Lord, to God our Savior, who daily bears our burdens" (Psalm 68:19).

God created the world, but He wanted more to love. Then, God created man. Fear not, trust in His love and that He sees and knows the path that you take. "The Lord watches over you - the Lord is your shade at your right hand; the sun will not harm you by day, nor the moon by night. The Lord will keep you from all harm - He will watch over your life; the Lord will watch over your coming and going both now and forevermore," (Psalm 121:5-8). He knows your heart as well, He knows what hurts you, He knows what makes you happy, He knows when you have done something wrong, and He knows your desires and passions as well. "If we had forgotten the name of our God or spread out our hands to a foreign god, would not God have discovered it since He knows the secrets of the heart?" (Psalm 44:20-21)

He knows the end from the beginning, and He has you covered! Just be still, be confident in Him, and trust Him to lead you to victory; He will not lead you astray. "Be still and know that I am God," (Psalm 46:10). You may not always understand the path, but in knowing that He always has you in His sight and has already been through ahead you should help you to trust Him more and have no fear of bad news or that you will fall along the way. "He will have no fear of bad news; his heart is steadfast, trusting in the Lord. His heart is secure, he will have no fear; in the end, he will look in triumph on his foes," (Psalm 112:7-8). God has had a plan all along for mankind; Jesus and He has had a plan for you too; all you need to do is to trust Him and be patient and wait on Him to fulfill it through you; keep studying His Word and above all, keep cherishing every moment you spend with Him. Yet the Lord longs to be gracious to you; He rises to show you compassion. For the Lord is a God of justice. Blessed are all who wait for Him!" (Isaiah 30:18)

He will get you through every trial victoriously and deliver you, so trust Him completely along the way knowing that if He allows something, He is only being a loving parent. It will be to teach you, draw an impurity out of you, or to impart a gift to you that you will learn through the situation. May God bless you as you begin your journey as a child of God and may He continue blessing you each and every day; remember, He has already been through ahead of you and He loved you enough to die for you; "He will never leave you nor forsake you."

Other Books by Sandra (Lott) Smith

Adult Books

Jeremy's Journey
Safe In Papa's Hands
Her Final Curtain
Deep Waters Within
Deep Waters Rage: Sequel to Deep Waters Within
My Father's Eyes: Seeing Yourself Through The Eyes of Love
Hannah's Journey To Purpose
Ride the Wind
An Eagle's Flight
A Princess in Waiting
The Princess in the Harlot
Step By Step Into A Deeper Walk In Christ
I'm Saved! Where Do I Go From Here?
The Day Hope Was Born: God's Gift of Love
The Holy Spirit and the Baptism of the Holy Spirit
Repairing Broken Walls: Restoring Joy & Peace-The Book
Repairing Broken Walls: Restoring Joy & Peace-The Study Guide
Jewels From the Word & Manna For the Soul
Captivated By God's Love: Poems From the Heart
You've Got This: Learning To Let Go
I'm Saved! What Next? Beginning Your Walk In Christ
The Father He Never Knew He Needed
In the Garden with Jesus
Princess Anastasia & the Kingdom of Divulgence

Children's Books

The Sheep That Went Astray
Naomi's Joy
Molly's Journey to Forgiveness
Tim & Gerald Ray Series: The Wind Has a Voice
Tim & Gerald Ray Series: How Did He Get in There?
Tim & Gerald Ray Series: A Light in the Sky
Tim & Gerald Ray Series: Let's Go Swimming
Tim & Gerald Ray Series: Blowing in the Wind
Tim & Gerald Ray Series: Summer on Grandma's Farm
Sassy Goes Exploring

Sandra (Lott) Smith was born and raised in San Antonio, Texas, with one sister and two brothers. Sandra loves the mountains, making candles, and jewelry. She is the author of Jeremy's Journey, Deep Waters Within, A Princess in Waiting, Ride the Wind, and more. She has also written children's such as, The Wind Has a Voice and How Did He Get in There, Molly's Journey to Forgiveness, and more. She has written over 39 books to date and began writing poetry as soon as she was saved in June 1998. The Lord gave her, her first book to write right after her son was killed. Writing was not something she sought out. She poured her heart into time spent with the Lord in order to allow Him to heal her heart and the name of her first book was birthed in her spirit along with the chapters and what it was to be about during a devotion time. It was called: God's Love; ironically enough, with all that she was going through, God's love was exactly what she needed.

She is passionate about studying the Bible. She has taught Sunday school, and Bible Study Groups, assists in preaching in her present church, and served in the Celebrate Recovery Ministry, and Homeless Outreach. Sandra was also interviewed on radio shows such as Golden Life Living and WMAP Radio (World's Most Amazing People based out of New York), the Bill Martinez show, and a Fox Radio show called the Kim Kennedy Show.

She is a devoted mother of 2 sons (Tim & Gerald Ray), Gerald Ray the youngest, has gone on to be with the Lord due to a car accident. Through the death of her youngest son at the age of 16, a rocky marriage to an alcoholic and the abuse that came with that, and other overwhelming trials, she has drawn close to the loving arms of the Father. Experiencing God's unconditional love as He held her heart in His hands, has created a passion in her to help others grow in their understanding of and receive God's love and grow spiritually. She has the heart to help hurting women discover the princess in Christ that they truly are and overcome abuse.

She teaches on topics to help you reach spiritual maturity, persevere through the hard times, and how to reach your destiny in Christ!